MESSY TOGETHERNESS

Published by
The Bible Reading Fellowship
15 The Chambers, Vineyard
Abingdon OX14 3FE
United Kingdom
Tel: +44 (0)1865 319700
Email: enquiries@brf.org.uk
Website: www.brf.org.uk
BRF is a Registered Charity

ISBN 978 0 85746 461 3

First published 2016
10 9 8 7 6 5 4 3 2 1 0

Acknowledgements
Scripture quotations from the Contemporary English Version. New Testament © American Bible Society 1991, 1992, 1995. Old Testament © American Bible Society 1995. Anglicisations © British & Foreign Bible Society 1996. Used by permission.

Scripture quotations taken from The Holy Bible, New International Version (Anglicised edition) copyright © 1979, 1984, 2011 by Biblica. Used by permission of Hodder & Stoughton Publishers, an Hachette UK company. All rights reserved. 'NIV' is a registered trademark of Biblica. UK trademark number 1448790.

Scripture taken from the Holy Bible, New International Reader's Version®. Copyright © 1996, 1998 Biblica. All rights reserved throughout the world. Used by permission of Biblica.

Scripture quotations from The New Revised Standard Version of the Bible, Anglicised edition, copyright © 1989, 1995 by the Division of Christian Education of the National Council of the Churches of Christ in the United States of America. Used by permission. All rights reserved.

Cover photo: © Ian Leadbetter

Every effort has been made to trace and contact copyright owners for material used in this resource. We apologise for any inadvertent omissions or errors, and would ask those concerned to contact us so that full acknowledgement can be made in the future.

A catalogue record for this book is available from the British Library

Printed and bound by CPI Group (UK) Ltd, Croydon CR0 4YY

MESSY TOGETHERNESS

BEING INTERGENERATIONAL IN MESSY CHURCH

MARTYN PAYNE

CONTENTS

FOREWORD

As the third worship song came to an end, a banner message flowed across the screen at the front: 'Children and young people should leave now.' At this, and with a fair amount of scuffling, squeezing and running down the aisles, the children and young people went. While a few of the adults left may have felt some relief at the quiet and calm that replaced the hubbub, most people could feel and sense the awkward emptiness. No longer were people squeezed together; no longer was there discussion, laughter and the buzz of creativity; instead there was a dull silence and a deep inner sense that something was missing. There was a gap…

The church community and church family are very precious, and we build up barriers between family members at our peril. To lose the joy of worshipping together regardless of age is damaging to the health of any church.

One of the many joys of Messy Church is the way that it has succeeded in crossing generational boundaries and encouraging people to worship together as individual families and as a 'church' family. This goes against the separation culture that the church has inherited, and instead shows that what we have been used to doing may not be the best thing to do.

In this book, Martyn Payne has brought together a compelling mix of thinking and resource. Based on his vast experience in both leading and observing Messy Church 'togetherness' in worship, he is able to identify the issues clearly and provide ideas, principles to work to, and session outlines that are eminently practical and useful. He also brings in some helpful theology, particularly exploring what 'family' meant in the broad context of Old and New Testament scripture. Then he adds in much of the recent and current thinking about what all-age worship is and could be, applying it to the Messy context and challenging some of the preconceptions about children and their spiritual growth. Martyn argues with his characteristic considered passion that we can and should be able to grow, worship and learn together and from each other, and we have a duty to make it happen.

This book is a great resource for the whole church. It is an invaluable tool for all those who are committed to Messy Church or are considering it. It is essential reading for those who lead worship in any church. It is also ideal for everyone, across our denominations, who has an inner sense that, when the children and young people leave, there is a gap, and we need to bring change.

Nick Harding
Children's Ministry Adviser
Diocese of Southwell and Nottingham

INTRODUCTION

Messy Church is the child in the midst of inherited church, playing, wondering, disturbing and questioning everything.

Since the first appearance of Messy Church over a decade ago in the UK, it seems that everything has been thrown up in the air. I mean this in a good way, because so much of what we have accepted as normal in the way we do church, go about our evangelism, make disciples and teach the faith does need to be re-examined in our day. Messy Church has allowed us to do this in a non-threatening way, since this fresh expression of church has grown up within the established structures and denominations of church, thus giving congregations the opportunity to compare and contrast what works and what needs to be reimagined when it comes to sharing and living out the gospel of Jesus Christ in the 21st century.

Discipleship, teaching and learning, children's and youth work, the sacraments and even church itself have all come under the Messy microscope, allowing us to ask playful but sometimes painful questions about the status quo. Messy Church is not, however, about throwing everything out and starting again. It's simply about taking a fresh look at what we have been doing and gently wondering whether some of our church methodology is still fit for purpose. As part of this investigation, one of the key areas in which Messy Church has pioneered a relatively new approach is the question of what it means to be church all together, all the time—in a messy togetherness where all generations learn with and from each other.

This book focuses on the 'all-age' value of Messy Church. Why do more and more people advocate the idea that the generations should develop their faith together, and what does the Bible have to say about it? How does this fit with our inherited model of age-related groups for learning and discipleship? Is it really practical and possible to have an experience of church in which the youngest to the oldest share the same meeting space, service theme and time to worship? Messy Church is claiming that this can and does happen.

Messy Togetherness is part of a series that the BRF Messy Church team has produced, taking a good look at the five key values of Messy Church—namely, hospitality, celebration, all-age, creativity and Christ-centredness. My aim in this book is to put the intergenerational claim itself under the microscope. In Part One I explore why we do it, and in Part Two I look at how being an intergenerational church can work out in practice, focusing particularly on the Messy Church model. In addition, the book includes three outlines for Messy Church sessions that focus on the theme of sharing faith when the whole body of Christ is together, drawing on stories from the Old and New Testaments.

Throughout the chapters ahead of you, you will find many references to particular Messy Churches that I have visited. Over the last three years, I have had the privilege of being a listener on behalf of the Messy Church movement, which has involved joining in with Messy congregations up and down the UK. This means that I have heard first-hand the stories of Messy Churches who are daring to explore what Messy togetherness means. My listening has been invaluable, enabling me to learn from some amazing Messy Church teams and leaders, and then go away and reflect more deeply on how Messy Church can better fulfil its all-age aspiration.

My visits have also, I am assured, been an encouragement to Messy Church teams. Those who work tirelessly and faithfully with children and families have often done so with little recognition, on the margins of many of our inherited churches. To be able to join with these Messy saints and both pass on ideas and go away inspired with fresh insights has been a blessing to me as much as, I hope, it has been for them.

The idea that church is not just desirable but better when all ages are together has, as you may imagine, not been received with universal enthusiasm. Of course, Messy Church proponents are not saying that this is the only way that church should ever be done. We do need like-minded groups to help our faith grow, and those groups are often age-related. However, to miss out on the significance and worth of doing faith intergenerationally does a huge disservice to a biblical understanding of how faith is passed on and how faith 'sticks' for each one of us. For this reason, the Messy togetherness 'banner' needs to be flown especially high for a time, at least in order to redress the imbalance in our approach to sharing and nurturing faith in our churches and communities.

Let me finish with a short story—not my own, but taken from a resource written by the founder of Messy Church, Lucy Moore. It comes from the 2014 Messy Month material that is still available.[1] It's a parable, and, as such, it exaggerates to make its point and argue the case for Messy togetherness. I hope it makes you smile, as it did me, but that it also opens up the question of the value of Messy togetherness, without which something is definitely missing in our experience of our Christian faith.

Once upon a time, a person—we'll call him Malcolm—had a huge, safe, beautiful house with a lovely garden. Malcolm decided to have a family to fill the house. But he decided he would choose exactly who would go in his family.

Malcolm was a man, so he decided there would only be men in his family.

Malcolm had black hair, so he decided he would just have men with black hair in his family.

Malcolm liked playing ping-pong, so he decided there would only be men with black hair who liked playing ping-pong in his family.

Malcolm was rich, so he decided only men with black hair who liked playing ping-pong and who were rich would be in his family.

Malcolm was British, so he decided that only men with black hair who liked playing ping-pong and who were rich and British would be in the family.

Malcolm liked cauliflower-flavour crisps, so he decided that only men with black hair, who liked playing ping-pong, were rich and British, and liked cauliflower-flavoured crisps would be in the family.

Malcolm was 38 years old, so... well, you can guess the rest!

So there they were, the very special, very happy, very exclusive family of 38-year-old British rich men with black hair, a ping-pong table in the living-room and plenty of strange crisps in the kitchen. But when Malcolm looked round at his family of male, black-haired, ping-pong-playing, rich, British, strange-crisp-eating 38-year-olds, he knew instinctively that something wasn't right.

'Something is not right!' he said to his family. 'What are we going to do with the other packets of crisps in the multipack? How will we all fit around the ping-pong table at once? What will happen when one of our family's hair turns grey... or falls out?'

The black-haired ping-pong players looked at each other in horror. 'And,' continued Malcolm, 'what about all the people who would enjoy being part of this family, who would love to learn to play ping-pong and who could enjoy the things that our money can buy? What about the fun we would have if different people joined us—people who are 28 or 8 or 98? People who are women or children? People who would love being in this huge, safe, beautiful house with its lovely garden? People who might eat up the other flavours of crisps?'

The family looked at each other. And they talked in little groups. And they decided... well, I wonder what you think they decided. Do you think they decided to let everyone else into the family, even though those people were different from them? Or do you think they decided to stay safe and cosy as they were? I wonder how hard it was to make that decision.

Here's to choosing Messy togetherness and the blessings of being intergenerational church.

PART 1

MESSY TOGETHERNESS AND WHY WE DO IT

CHAPTER 1

ALL TOGETHER NOW: IT'S WORKING

The background to all-age Messy Church

Of course they never arrive on time. But how could they? Gathering the Messy Church family together is never easy.

There's Jordan, who comes with his nan: they're always the first. And Liz, who brings her own two, plus three of the neighbour's children: she's a registered childminder. It takes her a while to sort everyone out, as well as park and unload the buggies. Then there's grandad Stan. He brings the whole family—daughter Jess with Peter and Alice, as well as his son's family. Quite a dynasty! They are always the first to get stuck into the crafts, barely stopping to be registered sometimes.

There's a new family here today. They only live round the corner and heard about us from Brenda, who helps at Mums and Tots. She's there too, of course, with her Lilly and Sean, as well as big brother John this time—to help, he says. Aesha is here again with her family. They've not missed a single Messy Church in two years and are virtually part of the team now. She always stays to help clear up. The two Jones sisters are here most months; both are single and in their 40s. They love coming. They say it's like being part of a big family and they always have a go at everything.

Dave, Brian and Gary are regulars on the team. They don't usually get involved with the crafts, but give them a practical job and you can be sure it will be done. Grandma Wendy is already out in the kitchen. She likes to be helpful. Oh, and there's Helen, who used to work at the school over the road. She knows most of the families, which is always a bonus for first-timers.

I suppose it takes at least 40 minutes, on a good day, but eventually the Messy family is gathered. New friendships are being made and others deepened; there's a buzz of conversation at the tables, with news being shared alongside chat about the Bible story. A young child is crying over by the soft play area but there are plenty of people around to come and comfort him. And so by the time the celebration time arrives, we are all together. We feel at home again; it's a safe place; it's a holy space. Our Messy family is laughing, learning and loving each other into the kingdom of God. Our intergenerational Messy Church is becoming a family, with children in the midst, who help us all to explore, to create, to discover and to question together. And Jesus is with us.

Every time our all-age family comes together like this, it's like a new beginning. It's something worth celebrating. And what's next? Well, we sit down and eat together, of course.

A SURPRISING NEW WAY OF BEING CHURCH

So another Messy Church gets underway, and those of you involved with running one of the many thousands of Messy Churches, either as leaders or as team members, will no doubt recognise my short semi-biographical sketch of what it's like at one of these fresh expressions of church for the 21st century. What's surprising, though, is that something like this is happening daily and in many different sorts of communities up and down the UK and around the world. Messy Church has gripped the imagination of Christians from a wide variety of denominations and traditions, so that it has become the largest church growth phenomenon in the recent history of the Western church. But perhaps even more surprising is just how simple, down-to-earth and unassuming this Messy revival is.

Messy Church offers an uncomplicated formula for reimagining church as a safe meeting place for those with faith and those for whom faith is almost the last thing on their minds. It's a shape of church that is not defined by what works for those who already believe but starts instead where people are. Messy Church is a way for Christians to show practical love and welcome to the wider community on their doorstep and to share what God means to them, not from a position of superiority but on a level plain of Messy togetherness. With its creative mix of crafts and activities, storytelling and song, conversation and a shared meal, Messy Church has made faith-sharing possible for thousands of ordinary Christians who have never felt qualified to be evangelists in our inherited understanding of that word. Messy Church has put a smile back on what it means 'to come to church' so that it has become an experience of shared laughter and friendship, where people meet with Jesus as they meet with those who already love and follow him.

THE ALL-AGE DIMENSION

There's one additional surprising thing about Messy Church. Although we have always known that doing things in community is a good thing, for some reason much of church history, particularly since the Reformation, has been marked by a segregated model of faith-sharing and discipleship. We have inherited a tradition of telling others about Christ in age-related and homogeneous social groupings. We have behaved as if true spiritual awakening can come only with age or alongside people who are like us.

Of course, it may well be easier to do it this way, but that doesn't make it right. As any teacher will tell you, it would be so much easier if all the students in front of him or her were starting in exactly the same place and with the same enthusiasm to learn; but that's not the real world. It is also not true when it comes to matters of faith. When sharing the good news of God's love to us in Jesus, a young child can be every bit as much alive to the Spirit of God as someone with a much longer experience of life. There are no age restrictions when it comes to 'tasting and seeing that the Lord is good'. It stands to reason, then, that the old have as much to learn from the young in the kingdom of God as the child has to learn from the adult.

TWO-WAY LEARNING

Many of you reading this will have had a long experience of working with children's groups in churches. Until recent years, the majority of programmes designed for supporting this ministry have assumed that it's the grown-ups who have something to share with the children. While there is truth in that, there has been a growing awareness, especially as research into children's spirituality has become more widely known, that the children can also be givers in this process, not just receivers. Consequently, children's work has very gradually moved from being a ministry that delivers and presents material *to* children to one that explores and discovers *alongside* them.

These insights should never have taken us by surprise. Jesus himself comments on the reality of the faith of 'these little ones' in his sayings about children, but, unfortunately, these sayings have been largely relegated to the footnotes of much of our theological thinking.

This rediscovery of the truth of God at work in everyone, at whatever age, has been vital to the DNA of Messy Church. Messy Church is unashamedly all-age. It's not just a children's activity or a special event only for families with preschool children; rather, it seeks to rediscover the intergenerational way in which faith is passed on from child to adult as much as from adult to child.

Messy Church takes this insight even further. It's not just that the children can help adults to see more of God but that the strangers we welcome into Messy Church can help us on our spiritual journey as much as we hope to help them. This further dimension might be hard to take for those of us who have been brought up with an 'us and them' approach to the gospel and the way we share it. However, if we revisit our Bibles prepared to unlearn as well as relearn, we will discover that Jesus found faith in unexpected people and places, just as the first Christians were compelled eventually to recognise God at work outside their Jewish boundaries. God is far bigger than the convenient boxes we want to confine him to.

MESSY TOGETHERNESS

In this context, Messy Church becomes, at its best, a melting pot of glorious messy togetherness. Children are in the midst, both to open our eyes to the wonder of the world and to keep our feet firmly on the ground in the realities of life. Strangers are in the midst, opening our vision to the way other people see things, with their honest questions about the challenges they face in their lives. Teenagers are in the midst, full of restless discontentment, questioning our inherited cultural norms and giving us fresh eyes to see the pressing issues of our day. Adults at all stages of life are in the midst, with their messy experiences and their messy journeys of faith, which can give us new perspectives on who we are in God.

This is a rich togetherness for faith development. This is a rich formula for Messy discipleship. This is a new way of being church which is not a new way at all, really. It is exactly how faith was always passed down from generation to generation, not by separating the generations off but by being together in the same space, sharing stories, experiences and life together.

Messy togetherness is arguably one of the most important strengths and gifts that Messy Church has for the church at large. Where the generational connections have become broken, we have seen faith falter. No wonder there's such a huge difference today between the growing churches of the majority world and the traditional churches of the West. I want to explore this exciting, challenging and significant value of Messy Church, arguing urgently that we must not lose this dimension but should strive with all our energy to make sure we stay intergenerational in every aspect of our togetherness.

THE PURPOSE OF THIS BOOK

The importance of this Messy Church all-age value is still very much contested. There are those who will argue strongly that separation and segregation remain important for many aspects of our Christian mission and ministry. I want to look at those arguments and investigate their validity. During my time working for The Bible Reading Fellowship (BRF), and within its Messy Church team in particular, I have had the opportunity to visit and be part of Messy togetherness in a huge variety of Messy Churches around the UK. Some Messy churches have embraced the all-age value brilliantly, while others struggle to do so. I recognise the huge temptation to give up on being intentionally all-age, and I hope to offer some ways forward for Messy Churches who are struggling to set up activities, run a celebration or provide the meal in a truly inclusive way for everyone present.

Our BRF Messy Church team is passionate about the all-age dimension. We sometimes joke about having the words 'all-age' tattooed on our foreheads! We believe that this aspect of Messy Church is particularly prophetic for the church in the 21st century, and we are not alone. For this reason, we do not want to compromise on what we believe the Spirit is saying to us as a church through this renewed awareness of the value of intentional togetherness.

In addition, to put my money where my mouth is, this book includes three fully worked-out Messy Church sessions that draw on Bible stories highlighting how special it is when all God's people, as the psalmist reminds us, 'live together in unity' (Psalm 133:1, NIV). Incidentally, the writer goes on to say that such togetherness is 'like precious oil… running down on Aaron's beard, down on the collar of his robe' (v. 2), or 'the dew of Hermon… falling on Mount Zion' (v. 3). This sounds very messy to me! But at the same time it is declared to be a blessing for everyone. So messiness and blessing do go together, and our messy togetherness in Messy Church is certainly one way God is blessing his world at this time.

FOR REFLECTION

- What has been your experience of Messy Church, if any?
- How have you experienced both separateness and togetherness on your journey of faith?
- How do you assess the effectiveness of passing on the faith at your own church?

CHAPTER 2

BRINGING THE GENERATIONS TOGETHER: IT'S IMPORTANT

Encountering difference

The Messy Church experiment began over a decade ago now and is, in many ways, very ordinary. It means consulting the community to find a better and more convenient day and time for those who might consider coming. It means intentionally using a more creative approach to learning, so that the biblical text is explored not through a sermon but through a range of hands-on activities, crafts, games and challenges. It includes a short gathered celebration time (the word 'celebration' being used because it makes more sense to a generation of people who may not relate to the word 'worship'), which comprises telling the Bible story in a creative, interactive way; singing something easy to learn; and giving space for some prayer and reflection. Finally and most importantly, there is a meal-time when friendships can be built as well as stomachs filled.

The constituent parts of this experiment are not particularly innovative, although putting them all together and calling it 'church' certainly is. To the founding team's surprise, this simple pattern of doing church differently took off and, like the mustard seed in Jesus' parable (Matthew

13:31–32), has become a huge, untameable tree, spreading out in surprising directions and becoming a home for all sorts of birds. Messy Church is now one of the most well-known fresh expressions of church in the UK. BRF, via its Messy Church website, is receiving on average one new registration every single day and, at the time of writing, there are just over 3200 Messy Churches recorded. Anecdotally, there are probably at least double that number, if we count those who haven't registered.

When I joined BRF's Messy Church team, one of my tasks was to visit and see what was happening on the ground in Messy Churches up and down the country. I was given the brief of spending time with Messy teams and congregations and simply enjoying what was going on in any particular Messy Church I visited. I met and talked with the leaders as well as those who turned up on the day; and, importantly, I spent time with the children and young people, listening to what they had to say. I have now been to over 130 Messy Churches and worked alongside teams from as many again, collecting a wide range of reflections and thoughts about how this missionary movement is developing.

NOT JUST FOR CHILDREN AND CARERS

From the outset, Messy Church has primarily reached out to young adults with their children. It is a church trying to engage with local families who are new to faith and new to church. However, I must add that Messy Church in my experience is definitely not just a church for children and their carers. It was always conceived as an all-age community, including older people who enjoy being around children, learning with and from them; single people who have found a place where they can belong and serve because church is speaking the language of their everyday lives; and both young and old from different family groups who rub shoulders together and learn something of what God's love looks like in a human person alongside them.

This bringing together of the generations is, in many ways, countercultural to the way church has been in recent centuries. Church at its best is one of the few organisations where you can find representatives from every age of life, from the babe in arms to the nonagenarian in a wheelchair. In fact, one of the very first Messy Churches I helped with in north London proudly took a photo of just such a pairing at their first session and entitled it 'From 9 months to 91'. But why is this so important?

THE DESIRE FOR COMMUNITY

It is widely acknowledged that the individualism that is now so much a mark of our Western society has had serious consequences for our sense of identity and our concern for our neighbour. Whatever benefits a wealthier lifestyle may have brought, there is no doubt that the 'me-generation' at the end of the 20th century and the 'selfie-generation' that we experience today have contributed hugely to the breakdown of face-to-face community. Individuals may have friends, but largely of the remote kind, on various forms of social media. Family members may still live together but often have separate existences, with televisions and computers enabling independent lives even under the same roof. Older people are particularly susceptible to isolation, because greater social mobility has meant that their extended families often live far away. No longer are relatives living within streets of each other or even within the same town.

There are, of course, exceptions to this pattern but, on the whole, our improved education system has allowed greater freedom for people to travel and even to pursue careers overseas. This has offered opportunities that take children far away from their roots, leading to loneliness and a disconnection between people that is becoming the norm. No wonder a community event such as Messy Church, just like the street party for a royal occasion, is attractive to so many people, and would be so even if there were no religious content.

ENCOUNTERING DIFFERENCE

In place of a truly diverse community, individuals generally choose to gather with those who share the same passions and interests. People network with disparate but like-minded groups who may not live anywhere near each other. There is nothing intrinsically wrong with this, but what gets lost is the opportunity to encounter difference in a safe place. Messy togetherness in a Messy Church is all about coming alongside each other, with all our messy differences, and I believe that this is a way towards both human and spiritual maturity.

Messy togetherness is a catalyst that may enable us to become the best we can be. In the second creation story in Genesis, God declares that it is not good for human beings to be alone (Genesis 2:18). That dilemma is solved by the creation of a partner who is equal to but different from the first human being. There is a deep truth here about human nature, which, Genesis also tells us, is modelled on God's own character, for it is created 'in his likeness' (1:26). God is also community. God declares from the outset, 'Let *us* make mankind,' and that difference-in-oneness is explored in the Christian doctrine of the Trinity—the ultimate three-in-one mystery. We flourish and are fully human (which is to be truly holy) when we enjoy and share in this same intimate experience with difference.

I can honestly say that, on my own Christian journey, I have learnt more by meeting difference than by sitting comfortably with sameness. Of course it is challenging, and sometimes even painful, to have to see things from another person's very different point of view, particularly when that person is also a believing Christian—but that's the point. This encounter of like with unlike is at the heart of bringing the generations together. The perspective of someone who has lived through the war in the 1940s or the sexual revolution in the 1960s, is very different from that of a young person who is a 21st-century digital native and for whom the keyboard is their third hand, but they both need each other to enrich their lives.

There is a growing awareness of the need for this intergenerational encounter. We see it sometimes in school programmes where retired adults from the local community come in to help with reading and work alongside children in the classroom, or at a community-focused charity event or project, such as a local food bank, where the age groups are brought together in a shared good cause. Contrary to the popular saying, wisdom is not always only passed 'down' but can also be passed 'across' the generations, and this is especially true of spiritual wisdom. It's this sort of pan-generational experience of togetherness that Messy Church offers.

LIMINAL PLACES

I would go as far as to say that bringing together the generations in this sense is a liminal encounter. You have perhaps come across the idea of 'thin places', where God seems to be particularly present. These are often sacred spaces on the margins—between the sea and the land, for example—perhaps out on an island such as Iona or Lindisfarne, or up a mountain where the earth 'touches' the sky. It was to just such a place that Jesus took three of his disciples when he wanted to reveal to them more of who he was. You can read about it in the story of the transfiguration (Mark 9:2–8). These can also be described as liminal places—places where there is a threshold, or crossing place, between different elements. In my experience, the same possibility of encounter with God is especially present when the old come alongside the very young, when a child walks alongside an adult, and when people of different backgrounds and outlooks find themselves together in a safe place such as Messy Church.

It's easy for our churches to become comfortable, cosy places of sameness rather than energising spaces that can hold together creative differences. In my experience, God often uses the latter to surprise us into new thinking and new insights on our faith journey. When I worked for the Church Mission Society (CMS), I often saw this happen for the young people who stepped into another culture overseas for a period of time, to work alongside a local mission partner or on a church project. They went out thinking that they were going to change the world, but came back realising that the greatest change was in themselves—and, of course, this *is* the way God changes the world.

EVEN MORE DIFFERENCE

The 'difference dimension' in Messy Churches can be huge. Not only are the generations all together, with their wide spectrum of perspectives, but Messy Church is also where many churches are truly meeting 'the world' for the first time. They have opened their doors and welcomed the community into the safe place they have created in Messy Church and, as a result, Christians are sitting alongside people from other faiths or no faith at all, or even those hostile to faith. However, this place of 'faith on trial' offers us the opportunity to encounter God afresh in surprising ways.

On my visits to Messy Churches, it's been interesting to note how some teams have recognised this dimension and found ways to receive, from the Messy Church guests, the gifts that they bring. I think back to one visit where the leaders were taken by surprise but, thankfully, were open to learn. Two families came for the first time. One woman had a child with special needs and she knew Makaton, so she offered to sign some of the songs and the Bible story, not just for her own child but for everyone there. During the meal, another new mum, who was Muslim by upbringing, brought a birthday cake for her child, which she wanted to share with the others in Messy Church. It became their unexpected dessert for the meal.

It was so good that the Messy Church was willing to receive these gifts in this way. When people feel valued, they flourish, and this is one way we can bless our guests in Messy Church. To take part and to have some ownership in the proceedings is possible in so much that happens in a Messy Church. Around the activity tables, during the celebration and at the meal, there is plenty of scope for this sort of belonging to begin to happen. But it can do so only when we understand Messy Church as a place of being alongside people as messy equals, rather than being there simply to deliver something to others. This is another aspect of Messy togetherness that Messy Church is slowly teaching us.

MODELLING FAITH

If we want to see our Christian faith caught and nurtured today, those with faith need to be alongside those who are learning faith. The young need to be alongside the old so that they can hear and learn from those with experience of trusting God in all the ups and downs of life. The old need to be alongside the young, who can bring the gift of a lively spirituality and an eager sense of adventure when it comes to exploring the wonders of God's creation and what faith in Jesus means. The friend needs to be alongside the stranger, who can show new ways of seeing and, ultimately, new ways of encountering God. Faith grown in this sort of liminal Messy Church soil is much more likely to put down deep roots and produce lasting fruit.

FOR REFLECTION

The leading American thinker and author on faith development, John Westerhoff III, has said, 'We grow by being with a group of people who are different from each other.'[2]

- What has been your experience, positive or negative, of encountering difference?
- Where do you have an experience of difference within your church?
- What stories of your own faith journey are associated with meeting difference?
- Can you think of a time when you unexpectedly came close to God as you walked alongside a child or a stranger?

CHAPTER 3

PASSING ON OUR FAITH: IT'S IN THE SCRIPTURES

Understanding Old and New Testament families

The opening verses of Psalm 78 have long been a rallying cry for those of us involved with children's ministry down the years: 'We will tell... the next generation. We won't keep secret the glorious deeds and the mighty miracles of the Lord' (Psalm 78:4).

I remember first hearing these words almost 40 years ago from a Scripture Union evangelist at our church. He was urging us to take children's ministry seriously and pass on the story of Jesus sincerely and passionately. Of course, he was right to underline the importance of this work. As has often been said, the church is only one generation away from extinction. If we don't tell our children about God's love and the story of Jesus, how will they ever come to a lively faith of their own? But these verses are challenging us to something even more fundamental. The psalmist is reminding us that faith needs to be taught and caught between the generations.

Faith in God is not learned in a theological hothouse, cut off from the experience of living out faith within the family. Coming to believe in God isn't just the result of a well presented and argued course in basic apologetics, however useful that might be in some contexts; rather, faith needs to be seen to be believed. Children need to see their parents practising what they believe; those parents may have learned how to pass on their faith from what was shown them by their parents, aunts and uncles, godparents and so on.

Families learn how to pray and why they pray by being alongside other families who are doing the same thing, and it can happen when those families meet up in an intergenerational congregation, such as at a special festival, on pilgrimage or when sharing a common experience of worship. This is exactly how the Jewish faith was passed on, as Psalm 78 tells us. The subsequent verses, which are not always read when this psalm is quoted, serve to underline what happens when the pan-generational experience of faith-sharing is forgotten. The psalmist reminds his listeners sadly that some of their ancestors didn't do this and so 'they broke their agreement with God' (v. 10) and were 'stubborn, rebellious and unfaithful' (v. 8).

STORYTELLING THE FAITH

The reminder to go on retelling the story at every opportunity sits at the heart of a scriptural experience of transmitting and holding on to faith. We often read the Old Testament through our New Testament eyes. We imagine that families came to faith because they were taught well by the priests at some sort of rabbinical Sunday school or during regular synagogue services. In fact, the synagogue was quite a late invention within the biblical narrative; it came about only when the people were in exile and the temple had been destroyed. Before then, faith was shared primarily within relational communities at home and at festival times.

If you asked someone from the tribes of Israel, during their long history, to tell you what God was like, they would immediately start telling a story: 'You see, once we were slaves in Egypt and we cried to God; God heard our cry and sent us a deliverer called Moses, who led us out of slavery through the waters to freedom. It was God who fed us in the desert and gave us the laws by which we live today…', and so the story would run. Their belief in God was rooted in their experience of God's love to them throughout the events of history. These are the stories that would have been told around the campfires in the desert and in the shade of the tent during the heat of the day. Those who remembered told those who had not yet heard, and they in turn passed the story on to others. The generations learned together.

This pattern was even more obvious when it came to festival times. Groups would re-enact moments from their story, whether the creation of booths in the desert for the Feast of Shelters or their amazing deliverance during the time of Esther at the feast of Purim. Most significantly, of course, they would relive their escape from Egypt at the Passover meal. The whole family would sit down and literally eat and drink the story, which was told in response to the youngest child's question, 'What does this night mean?'

TALK ABOUT GOD'S LAWS, ALL THE TIME

It was in this context that faith was taught and caught successfully, all through the pages of the scriptures. This is a dimension of faith-sharing that perhaps we have lost today, both because belief has become a privatised affair and because it is a Sunday-centred experience for large numbers of us, particularly in the Western world. We have abandoned the experience of faith storytelling across the generations and, as a result, we have dropped the baton of faith.

The shared togetherness of faith journeys, as exemplified in Old Testament practice, was so much part of the experience of God's people in the past that it was often taken for granted and did not get mentioned. That's unfortunate for us today because we desperately need reminding. Only now and again is it made explicit, in passages such as Deuteronomy 6:6–9, where the writer reminds us to walk and talk the faith alongside our children at home and along the road, when we are going to bed and getting up in the morning, and every time we go in and out of the doors of our home. It's significant that these instructions about how faith should be shared come straight after the great summary of the faith in verse 4, which is the closest we get to a credal statement of Jewish belief: 'Listen, Israel! The Lord our God is the only true God! So love the Lord your God with all your heart, soul, and strength.' The heart of faith can only be learned, it seems, in the heart of the home and in the context of the everyday life, where young and old work and live alongside each other.

OLD TESTAMENT 'FAMILY'

There is, however, another dimension to this issue, which is of particular interest as we work out what it means practically in the messy togetherness of Messy Church. Not only do we look back at the Old Testament with New Testament or 21st-century eyes and wrongly interpret how the faith was being learnt with and from each other, but we also read the story with so-called modern ideas of what these families of faith looked like. They were certainly nothing like the 'nuclear family' of our more recent history. Old Testament families included a wide network of immediate relatives and more distant ones who belonged to the same tribe; they linked up all who were connected not just by DNA but by bonds of friendship, financial obligation and mutual concern over territory and shared faith. They were a true messy togetherness of the elderly, married and single adults, children and stepchildren, all in the mix, spanning three or four generations. This is the context in which faith was shared and the young and old talked together about what God had done for them all.

It is interesting to reflect that we are moving towards this wider understanding of family in the 21st century. Many of us who run Messy Churches will recognise this bigger, messier family picture. At a new Messy Church I visited, on a large housing estate in the Midlands, I sat alongside a mum who had brought her family along. She wanted her children to hear something of the Christian story that she vaguely remembered as being important when she was very young, when she attended a Sunday school for a while. Her journey since then had been very messy, as she told me in great detail. She had with her a teenage son from her first marriage; also at the table were three primary-aged children from her second marriage, which had been cross-cultural. Her diverse family was typical of many at this Messy Church, where she felt accepted rather than judged, and welcomed rather than made to feel uncomfortable because of her circumstances. It was in this messy togetherness that she was hoping that faith could be taught and caught—something that, if left to her alone as a single mum at home, might never happen.

NEW TESTAMENT 'HOUSEHOLDS'

The wider understanding of messy families is one that we also often fail to recognise in the New Testament narrative. Households of faith in the early days of the church were much more diverse and mixed than we perhaps imagine. The mixture of people in a first-century home, in one of the cities of the Roman provinces where Christianity began to flourish, looked very different from the single-family households in our Western world. Instead, there was a completely different hierarchical understanding of the household, with the inclusion of people who were not blood relatives, such as slaves, freedmen and those to whom the *pater familias* would give patronage.

This was a much more open understanding of family than a 21st-century one, in which there was arguably less sentiment and more real, hard obligation, with legal, financial and moral implications in both directions. This was the intergenerational mix within which the first believers celebrated and shared their newfound faith in Christ. In fact, it was close to the concept of extended family that we find in the Old Testament; in both cases, this was the primary place in which faith was transmitted, nurtured and tested. Faith didn't depend on Sunday attendance and special times of outsourced teaching—which have become the dominant means for passing on our faith, particularly in the Protestant Church.

It's instructive also to take a second look at how Jesus himself formed a new community of faith around him. In contrast to normal practice in his day, the disciples did not choose to go and sit at the feet of this new young teacher from Nazareth; instead, in a move that was quite radical for the time, it was Jesus who chose who would walk alongside him and learn about the kingdom of God on pilgrimage together. In other words, this wasn't a gathered community in a school but a journey of learning in messy togetherness. The Gospel accounts reveal frequent differences of opinion among these first disciples—for example, in their attitudes to outsiders and their arguments over who was the greatest. Bringing together Galilean fishermen, a former tax collector and a local freedom fighter (Simon the Zealot) was extreme messy togetherness... but it worked.

TODAY'S MESSY FAMILIES

Messy Church is showing us a way of creating a sort of messy togetherness that more closely resembles the context in which faith was caught in both Old and New Testaments. Messy Church offers a safe public space where a new family that crosses the boundaries of DNA is formed. Most importantly, it goes one step further, opening this new church door to people who would previously never have set foot over the threshold, allowing them to meet the true heavenly *pater familias* in a messy household where each can find wholeness of body, mind and spirit.

On my travels, I have seen evidence of this again and again. Those who struggle with life are made welcome in the larger family community of Messy Church, which takes their needs seriously. People who are not particularly gifted and talented are encouraged to help on the team, and are thus helped themselves as much as they help others by their inclusion in the running of the Messy Church. Children find new spiritual godparents, aunties and uncles, who can help them see what believing in Jesus means as they sit and make things around a table, listen to stories together and enjoy food at the messy dining table. Old and young, who have grown up with no religious language to help them explore and express their spirituality, find in Messy Church models of specifically Christian practices to imitate at home, such as how to pray, how to read the Bible with others, how to say grace, and how to bless each other.

People learn best by having things modelled to them, and this is what is happening when messy togetherness is at the heart of being church. It has been fascinating, particularly in some more urban Messy Churches, to watch the evolution of behaviour and attitudes in the way people treat each other. Messy Church is acting as a gentle but firm parent to all ages, constructing and maintaining an environment that is helpful and wholesome for everyone, however old or young. Families are acting as models of parenthood and 'dutiful childhood' to each other, and deep learning is going on at a social as well as a spiritual level.

Messy Church is putting the responsibility for passing on and nurturing faith back into the hands of the parents, grandparents and significant Christian adults. This is why Messy Church insists so firmly that children do not come unaccompanied. Lucy Moore, the founder of Messy Church and leader of the BRF Messy Church team, put this very clearly in an e-mail to me:

Messy Church was conceived with this desire to bring Christ into the family pattern, not just into a child's pattern of life in isolation. This is in accord with the biblical imperative to share faith within a broad household of faith: all ages and social strands together under one Father and thus one clear vision for loving each other as he loves us. It's about demonstrating that faith goes on beyond the age of eleven. It's about expressing kingdom values and presence in the generosity of the activities and food; in the attitudes of the leaders and helpers who pour themselves out for even the most 'difficult' children—or adults, for that matter.

It's about the household, too, of the team that Messy Church demands, which says so much about what the body of Christ is about. It's about equality and justice and opening up the inner mysteries of faith to the lowest of the low, not keeping it to an elite who are 'trained' or, indeed, those who pay the bills. It's about children being at the centre and inviting adults to learn from and with children, but also to nurture the child within them who may never have had the chance to play or be loved.

SIGNIFICANT SPIRITUAL ADULTS

When I visit a Messy Church, it's not uncommon for me to become, at least for the two hours we are together, an honorary grandparent to some of the children I encounter. I am a safe adult in the mix of adults and children together. I am someone who can talk about faith with them, who isn't a relative or registered carer for that child. I am an elder brother who can listen and share my experience of my own messy faith journey as I also (humbly, I hope) listen to theirs.

Our current culture of heightened safeguarding has sadly become necessary because of the depraved inclinations of a tiny minority in our society who have abused the vulnerable—even within churches. We recognise the necessity for this awareness, but it has set up some unfortunate tensions with the strong need for children to feel comfortable alongside a wider family group than the nuclear family in which they have been brought up. As long as people are alert and aware of best practice—just as in any gathered community event—

there is no reason why, within Messy Church togetherness, we should not begin to rediscover a safe way to be alongside each other, across the generations and across some of the fearful divides that have pulled us apart. It's a togetherness that needs careful planning and watchfulness on the part of the team, but, where it works well, as I have seen in so many cases, the benefits are huge. There is a rediscovery of the biblical perspective on how we should talk about our faith in the everyday and pass it on in the ordinary events of life.

FOR REFLECTION

- What sort of family groups come to your church or Messy Church?
- How can your church or Messy Church best support these families on a journey of faith?
- Is our 21st-century Western culture just so different from the biblical world that genuine Messy togetherness across the generations is impossible to recreate? What are the barriers and what are the new possibilities in your experience?

CHAPTER 4

LEARNING FROM EACH OTHER: IT MAKES SENSE

Current thinking and practice on all-age faith development

The story of all-age worship and learning in UK churches has been a chequered one. Perhaps, like me, you have lived through the last 40 or so years of experiments in this area and still carry the scars! In many ways, it has been a story of knee-jerk reactions to current trends and statistics—in particular, falling attendance at Sunday services.

The traditional Sunday schools began to decline in number in the second half of the 20th century in Britain, as families were attracted by so many alternative things to do on a Sunday. There was also an increased questioning of traditional churchgoing, which meant that many young parents no longer saw going to church as 'the acceptable norm'; anyway, shouldn't their children be given space to make up their own minds about faith? All this seemed to take the church by surprise. Perhaps we had assumed that people would just go on believing and coming along, without any effort on the church's part to encourage it to happen. The result was a series of reactive bursts of new ideas and reorganisation.

FAMILY SERVICES

Sunday schools that had taken place in the afternoon were moved to the morning, in the hope that whole families would start coming back to church rather than parents just dropping off their children to have the story of faith explained to them by someone else. When this did not produce a rise in church attendance by families with children, churches adopted the monthly family service approach, which is still favoured by many churches today.

However, the problem was that no one really knew how to do a family service or even what it meant. Having the generations together in the same physical space is not the same as true intergenerational worship and learning. Many family services didn't look much different from what took place normally without the children, except perhaps for a token children's chorus or a special children's talk. No wonder children preferred to be in Sunday school, where there was someone who knew them by name and spent time listening to them and giving them a chance to participate. How could we have ever thought they would enjoy being stuck in a pew among a congregation of older, often unsympathetic adults and asked to sit through the majority of the service rather than being actively welcomed and included? Nevertheless, the experiment continued, with varying degrees of success, which depended heavily on the talents of those who were in leadership. Unfortunately, planning and leading such services has never been very high on the agenda of ministerial formation (if at all) and, as a result, many families began to vote with their feet.

THE ALL-AGE SERVICE

In order to rescue the situation, the family service morphed into the 'all-age service'. This sort of worship attempted to push the boat out further, in terms of adapting liturgy to be far more informal and to give much more opportunity for children in particular to feel at home with the language and content of the service. An abundance of resources labelled as 'all-age service resources' appeared towards the end of the 20th century, and there was certainly much good material in these books. Nevertheless, the tide of church decline, especially among young families with children, was not turned. The church continued to struggle to make itself accessible to a generation used to participation, interactivity and shared learning. Even the best of the all-age service experiments often failed to deliver these vital ingredients.

There have been several reactions to this challenging situation. Some churches have decided that a segregated approach is clearly still the best. Such churches have often been the larger ones, with better resources in terms of materials and people, running what are best called multi-generational congregations. There may be some occasional meeting together but, on the whole, faith sharing and faith nurture happen in separate groups. This model has sometimes even led to the development of separate children's and youth churches.

The big problem with this approach is that faith sharing is franchised out to others, not to the parents or carers at home. As we saw in our last chapter, the relational community approach to passing on the faith is the biblical model, and one of the consequences of pushing it to one side was that many children did not survive the 'siloed' approach to their faith development. They found support and nurture within their peer group, of course, but did not know how to relate to other age groups in the church when they all came together. For this group, maturing into adult worship as grown-ups themselves has proved difficult. There are notable exceptions, but, in my experience, most of those who survive do so where there has also been a strong faith at home to support their spiritual journey.

FRESH EXPRESSIONS

Another response to the all-age challenge has been to shake up the way we do church together even more radically. Some fresh expressions of church have experimented with a more discussion-based approach to biblical themes, including family activities as part of the service and involving whole family groups in the planning and delivery of the liturgy. There are some fine examples of this happening, although sometimes even here (especially within the more established churches) there are huge tensions between the new activities and expectations about what should be included in a service of worship, as well as what is possible if all ages are present. Key areas of conflict include the sort of hymns and worship songs that are used and, in particular, the way the Eucharist is celebrated reverently within this context. The Sunday morning slot for worship is being asked to carry a lot of expectations, so it is not surprising that it often fails to deliver, caught between conflicting hopes and fears.

All of this highlights a far deeper issue. There is really no point in pursuing even the most radical and exciting sort of all-age service if there has not been a shift in the whole culture of the church that is trying to make it happen.

'Intergenerational' is not something that churches do; it's something that they become.

AN INTERGENERATIONAL CULTURE

The need for a shift in culture was picked up in particular by CPAS (Church Pastoral Aid Society) around the turn of the millennium, at a time when CPAS had a much bigger involvement with children's and young people's ministry and it was beginning seriously to tackle the issue of all-age church. Pioneer thinking expressed at its conferences and training, as well as in the Grove booklet *Body Beautiful?*,[3] underlined this issue well. Unless churches began to reassess everything they did through an all-age lens, the once-a-month all-age worship was always going to be a challenge. There needed to be a paradigm shift in people's thinking about how to be intergenerational, in order to try to reproduce, in a small way at least, those biblical models of extended family where faith was passed on naturally across the generations rather than through the occasional service, however well that was done.

MESSY CHURCH

It was at this stage in the development of all-age worship that Messy Church in the UK was born. Right from the start, this fresh expression of church nailed its colours clearly to the mast: it was a church with an intergenerational culture as its heartbeat. About the same time, there was a reawakening in the UK to the importance of children's innate spirituality, which, in turn, opened eyes to the value of human spirituality. Rather than doing church to children and adults, we needed to find a new way to do church together, so that a sense of 'faithing' together on pilgrimage might be recovered. Messy Church was a response to this cry, with the added dimension that it recognised that the Sunday morning slot was no longer the most convenient time for families to come together in their busy week.

At the same time as this development in the UK, there was much new thinking about intergenerational ministry in the United States, where the separation of the age groups has increasingly been questioned by key theologians and writers. Children do not catch the faith well if it is only told to them in a separate age-related Sunday school environment. A number of research projects have highlighted the need for young people to receive support from non-parent adults and other people of faith from the congregation, across the different generations—adults who demonstrate that faith is for life, not just for Sunday school. Intergenerational ministry is, at its best, a ministry with and by the whole family of God, and this is what most benefits faith nurture for children and adults. Two of the leading writers in this field at the moment are Ivy Beckwith and David Csinos, who have written on this theme together as part of the Faith Forward movement. One paragraph from a recent journal article is particularly worth quoting, and I highlight some words in the middle with a wry smile:

Truth be told, much of what counts as congregational worship isn't terribly child-friendly (and sometimes it's not even adult-friendly). But when we experiment with new possibilities for congregational worship, we open the doors to forming practices that are inclusive of people of all ages. ***It may be messy****, but armed with a spirit of creativity and a willingness to make mistakes, faith communities can develop all sorts of practices in which the young and old can* *join together in worship, practices that nurture the spiritual lives of children—and of people of all ages.*[4]

Indeed it may be, and is, messy! Or perhaps we would prefer to use the word 'playful'. This playful or messy element is, of course, at the heart of Messy Church. Much of the discussion about intergenerational church in America has been in the context of reimagining Sunday morning worship. I feel that, in the UK, we have already travelled that road and are now in a different place. Much of what is advocated by these experts is good theory but, in fact, represents what is now being worked out in practice in Messy Church. Here, creativity is right at the heart of what is going on; there is a willingness to make mistakes, and practices are being developed where all ages can join together, nurturing the spiritual lives of all those involved.

NEW THINKING

All this rethinking about all-age practice is well documented in a range of research papers and books. Another leading theologian with a heart for the spiritual nurture of children is Beth Barnett from Australia, and, in an article in Premier's *Children's Work* magazine published in the UK, she argued for the importance of being together in worship as the way for faith to be passed on. She wrote, 'The different generations bring different contributions which meet the diversity of needs in one another far more effectively than in homogenous groups of consumers.'[5] She also argued that we have fallen out of the habit and lost many of the basic skills of simply being together. Years of doing things separately have had an unfortunate legacy within the church and it has taken a while to begin to find a new way forward.

The same thinking has emerged through the Sticky Faith movement.[6] This has come from the USA but has been taken up and promoted actively in seminars across the UK by Scripture Union in recent years. The argument is that if we want to have a faith that 'sticks' for children and young people, it means surrounding them with people of faith from all generations. Once again we are back to the biblical model, where faith was caught and taught because people did not live primarily as individuals but as part of extended families.

Another important contribution to this debate comes from the Lutheran practitioner and speaker Linda Staats, who reminds us that cross-generational ministry is a ministry of accompaniment and that our communities of faith have an untapped potential for bringing all generations together through all ages and stages of life. She intentionally creates her all-age worship around groups that bring together the generations, and suggests that the ideal number around a table is five differently aged people who together explore and share their stories of faith.

SILOED FAITH NURTURE

All this is not to say that the day of exclusive age-specific ministry is over. Clearly it does still have its place and is still working to varying degrees, but the truth is that it has not proven a sustainable model for the ongoing transmission of faith among those who have grown up exclusively with such siloed ministries. If it had, then we would not be facing the statistics of church decline that we do at present, particularly among the churches of the Western world. Churches have always been among the few places where families, singles, couples, children, teens, grandparents and all generations can come together on a regular interactive basis. We should be rejoicing in this and making it possible, rather than continuing to resort to ways to segregate by age those who come.

I find it interesting that, in this respect, the secular world is showing us the way, with an increasing emphasis on making things more family-friendly and family-inclusive in many areas of life. Of course, there's a market in it for the providers, but it is also a reflection of where people want to be. So you will find more family-friendly restaurants and pubs, family-friendly entertainment and activities, family-friendly holidays and accommodation, and adverts that play on the intergenerational experience of families loving the same product down the years. There is even, as I write, a new TV game show that deliberately builds on this intergenerational experience of family.

This is where Messy Church comes into its own. We are not just talking about a good idea on paper and a good theory about faith nurture and faith sharing; rather, we have a viable model of how it can work. It's all very well to have ideas about what should happen but quite another thing to offer a new wineskin of church where the theories can be worked out in practice. No wonder the take-up of Messy Church has been so overwhelming, and continues to be so!

Messy Church is unashamedly intergenerational. It's a model for being all-age that does not try to squeeze itself into the clothes of Sunday morning, only to find that that they are, at best, an uncomfortable fit; nor is it simply a special children's event, inviting parents along as spectators. At every level, Messy Church enables the messy creativity, conversations and learning together about our faith that many contemporary thinkers and writers are recommending. The children enjoy this form of church and the parents enjoy becoming children again alongside them. Children are meeting with other safe adults, outside their normal family circle; and those without children are experiencing a place of community, with the opportunity, should they want it, to become spiritual godparents to the next generation. One Anglican vicar posted the following comment on the BRF Messy Church Facebook page not long ago:

Our Messy Church was a response four years ago to many insights, including the fact that a whole generation of unchurched young parents were bringing babies for christening but felt that traditional church was a very alien place indeed. [Over the intervening years] the most astonishing thing we have learnt is that children tend to teach the adults: they have an uncluttered spirituality; they are welcoming and generous to newcomers; they are eager and open to learning; and their ability to be still and pray earnestly and with great devotion is inspiring. And the children bring their friends along! If only our Sunday congregations were as good as Messy Church at introducing friends to church, we'd be in great shape.

My own experience as a young parent is perhaps relevant here. I found it very hard to go to church, once our children were of Sunday school age, only to be expected to let them go off to their age-related activities. I didn't want to be separated from them, nor they from us, particularly in our boy's case. The result was something that some of you may recognise: I ended up going out too, helping with the Sunday group—and hence a children's ministry career was born!

I am still very uncomfortable to be in worship without

children. It's like having an important family meal but asking half the family members to eat elsewhere, often in a colder and less attractive room. It's like having a family holiday but leaving the children behind (although perhaps some of you would welcome this!). Of course I recognise that there are times when it's good to have some space. However, when it comes to the matter of passing on our faith, I would strongly argue that it is totally inappropriate. The faith of our children is too important to be siloed off and put at risk.

Faith sharing has always been a 'one-another' affair. It is something that can only be done in community, so we are instructed again and again in the early writings of the church to teach one another, serve one another, encourage one another and, above all, love one another. We can sometimes forget that when Paul wrote instructions like these, his words were being read out to the whole church, which included children and adults together. Any form of church that herds us into rows or prevents us from connecting with one another is holding us back from this messy but vital opportunity for faithful togetherness.

FOR REFLECTION

- What part has the intergenerational factor played in your journey of faith?
- How would you evaluate the model of faith formation at your church?
- What arguments for and against separateness in worship would you make from your experience?

CHAPTER 5

WHAT THE SPIRIT IS SAYING TO THE CHURCHES

Recent thinking on intergenerational ministry

The move towards messy togetherness hasn't just appeared out of nowhere in our generation. As I hope I have shown in the previous chapters, there is plenty of support from scripture and the history of the church to advocate bringing the generations together for worship and learning. In fact, only in recent centuries has our focus shifted towards passing on our faith in separate and homogeneous people groups. For most of us, in the Western church at least, the default position among all but the smallest churches has been to divide the congregation up, particularly by age, on the assumption that passing on spiritual truths needs a model drawn from the classroom. Yet the truth is that the spiritual curriculum has nothing to do with how young or old we are.

Throughout Christian history, there have been key moments of paradigm shift in our theological thinking—for example, the time when the Christian faith became the official religion of the Roman empire, the birth of the monastic movement, the Reformation and the Pentecostal movements of the 20th century. On these occasions, the Holy Spirit of God has spoken afresh to the church and God's people have responded, albeit slowly, by embracing new directions in their ministry and mission. The move towards messy togetherness is, I believe, another such *kairos* moment for the growth of God's kingdom on earth. Where separateness has been the default position for churches, with some occasional gathering together, togetherness is now slowly becoming the default again, with occasional times apart.

This change of perspective has been signposted by many writers and thinkers in recent years. In this chapter I have gathered a series of quotes and comments from current research and publications which support my contention that the Spirit is indeed speaking to the church in our generation. Do take some time to read each of the following extracts carefully and to reflect on what God may be saying to you concerning your own Christian congregation, in response to these insights about intergenerational ministry.

FROM MINISTRY PROFESSIONALS AND RECENT RESEARCH

There are three key recommendations from The Family Ministry Research report commissioned by the Consultative Group for Ministry among Children (CGMC, a network of Churches Together in Britain and Ireland) and The Methodist Church, published in September 2015.[7]

- Working with children or young people in isolation was not the most effective way of enabling a lifelong relationship with God... Nurturing spirituality needs to involve parents and a wider 'family', leading to a growing awareness around an all-age approach to church.

- It was identified that being part of a church congregation offered unique opportunities to meet with people of different ages and this aspect of being an intergenerational community was felt to be important.
- There is a cross-denominational, although not universal, direction of travel away from ministering to the church community in separate age groups and towards an integrated approach... where differing styles of worship and learning are accommodated, across all ages.

'Intergenerational ministry occurs when a congregation intentionally brings the generations together in mutual serving, sharing and learning within the core activities of the church in order to live out being the body of Christ to each other and the greater community. Throughout much of Christian history, the whole body of Christ—that is, all generations—met together for ministry and worship as well as most other gatherings; intergenerationality was the norm.'[8]

'The best way to be formed in Christ is to sit among the elders, listen to their stories, break bread with them, and drink from the same cup, observing how these earlier generations of saints ran the race, fought the fight and survived in grace.'[9]

'The church is the only agency in Western civilisation which has all the members of the family as part of its clientele... through the complete lifecycle from birth to death.'[10]

'The heart of intergenerational congregational life is to be found in the telling of stories.'[11]

'Intergenerationality has deep roots in a Jewish and Christian heritage. The call for one generation to share its faith and story with future generations is deeply embedded in the Jewish tradition.'[12]

'Churches have been among the few places where families, singles, couples, children, teens, grandparents—all generations—come together on a regular interactive basis. Yet, the societal trend toward age segregation has moved into churches also. Age-based classes for children as well as adults, teen programs, and separate worship services for adults and children tend to separate families and age groups from each other, so that children could experience religion as age-segregated throughout their lives.'[13]

'For too long, for instance, parents have "outsourced" the faith formation of their children to professional ministry leaders, instead of assuming the spiritual responsibility that is properly theirs. And for too long congregational leaders have regarded children's ministry and youth ministry as adjunct activities, sitting outside the "core" of church life and practice. Neither approach has served children, youth, families and congregations well! It is important for the future of faith formation that the relationships between the spheres of home, whole congregational life and age-specific programming are reimagined and reconfigured.'[14]

'I am convinced of this: the best way for children, youth and family ministry leaders to nurture our children and young people in faith is nurture their parents/caregivers in faith together with them. That means bringing parents and youth/children into the same places and spaces to hear and reflect together on God's word. That means inviting them to speak out their stories of faith with one another. That means trusting the Holy Spirit to be at work in and through whatever unscripted moments emerge along the way.'[15]

'The Search Institute found that what really makes a difference in a young person's life is not just whether or not a person receives support from nonparent adults, but the number of nonparent adults that support them. According to Search, three is the magic number. Receiving support, encouragement, and guidance from three or more nonparent adults is a key developmental asset. Through intergenerational community, children and youth have opportunities to form these types of relationships. This is relational ecclesiology, or a theology of church that's built on relationship.

'The challenge is, however, that family ministry is too often narrowly imagined and implemented by congregations. While scholars such as Diana Garland paint vivid images of the full breadth of family ministry, in the day-to-day realities of church life it can too often become seen as children's ministry with adults sitting in and it can leave single persons, couples without children, empty-nesters, and seniors on the sidelines. We dream of intergenerational community that embodies family ministry at its best—ministry with the whole family of God! We dream of children's ministry that benefits from the context of a church joined together rather than segregated by age.'[16]

'We have fallen out of the habit and lost many of the basic skills of being together.'[17]

'Intergenerational is not something churches do—it's something they become.'[18]

'The church is a partnership of generations fulfilling God's purposes in their time.'[19]

'The issue is this: yes, we can seem to learn more effectively and comfortably in segregated groups. But is learning what church is primarily about? If church is about loving God and loving each other and transforming the world in partnership with him and with each other, can we achieve that best by splitting up or learning to live together? If I cannot learn to cope with praying in church with a slightly smelly 80-year-old, a 15-year-old who is cleverer than I am, a toddler who wriggles or a woman who won't stop weeping, what hope do I have of loving people outside the church?...

'An all-age church reflects the very nature of a diverse yet unified God. It demonstrates the integration of generations to which society as a whole can aspire, thus challenging the worldview that splits off the generations from each other in fear and hostility. It is the way that Christians have celebrated their faith for centuries. It is the best way of growing disciples.'[20]

'The church which welcomes children, accepts their gifts and ministries, meets their needs, advocates justice and seeks new life with them, joins them in challenging evil with love and truth, continues to learn with and from them the values of the Kingdom by living them out, is a church which is good news not only for children and its adult members but for the world.'[21]

'Churches should be healing communities in which children play their part in the life of the whole... Churches should provide models of how to mediate between children and adults... Churches ought to support families as "little churches" with one of their priorities being to help parents be good ministers of the gospel in the home... Churches need to value and support worship outside church such as that at the meal table, on holidays or at bedtime—in this respect the Jewish balance between synagogue and home is very instructive.'[22]

'In the Bible all-age worship worked! Families worshipped together, communities prayed together and whole nations danced together in praise of God. When Miriam led all the people of Israel in a dance and song of celebration after they had escaped from Egypt through the Red Sea, children mixed with adults as all celebrated the love and power of God. Modern Jews look on the way the Christian church treats children with a mixture of sadness and mystification. If all-age worship worked centuries and millennia ago, there is no excuse for us not giving it a shot now!'[23]

'Churches should consciously set out to include all generations and enable them to relate meaningfully. As well as being racially and ethnically diverse... another diversity to be faced and overcome is that of age and generation... Perhaps one of the reasons some current attempts at all-age worship fail is that they are not born out of genuine intergenerational relationships, or an authentic "all-age culture" but rather the worship "service" is the only time everyone gets together in one space to do anything all together. {Philip] Mounstephen and [Kelly] Martin comment: "If all-age worship does not flow naturally from the integrated life of the community it is a sham." Rather than focusing on the worship service, they suggest the church needs to prioritise relationships and community in other ways, focusing on becoming an "all-age church" rather than simply a church with an all-age service.'[24]

'"Intergenerational" is the buzz word in the study of ageing. Massive international research programmes are devoted to intergenerational issues... A secular community development researcher recently asked one of us why the churches do not do more intentional intergenerational work. She observed that, in a society in which extended families are geographically dispersed, child care is outsourced and child-free resorts and retirement villages are becoming more common, the churches are among the few natural intergenerational spaces left to us. As so often, an outside perspective can illuminate a theological issue: her observation about the nature of churches resonated strongly with the vision of the kingdom of God. Here, old and young live side by side in peace, as part of a society where both genders and all races are also fully represented (Zechariah 8:1–8; Joel 2:27–29; Acts 2:7–18).'[25]

FROM THE BIBLE

> Praise him, young men and women. Praise him, old men and children. Let them praise the name of the Lord. His name alone is honoured. His glory is higher than the earth and the heavens. (Psalm 148:12–13, NIRV)

I appeal to you, brothers and sisters, in the name of our Lord Jesus Christ, that all of you agree with one another in what you say and that there be no divisions among you, but that you may be perfectly united in mind and thought. (1 Corinthians 1:10, NIV)

Blow the trumpet in Zion, declare a holy fast, call a sacred assembly. Gather the people, consecrate the assembly; bring together the elders, gather the children, those nursing at the breast. (Joel 2:15–16, NIV)

At that time the disciples came to Jesus and asked, 'Who, then, is the greatest in the kingdom of heaven?' He called a little child to him, and placed the child among them. And he said: 'Truly I tell you, unless you change and become like little children, you will never enter the kingdom of heaven. Therefore, whoever takes the lowly position of this child is the greatest in the kingdom of heaven. And whoever welcomes one such child in my name welcomes me.' (Matthew 18:1–5, NIV)

FOR REFLECTION

- Which of these quoted passages have particularly spoken to you about your own church situation?
- Which ones do you disagree with? Which would you interpret differently?
- Why not share some of these passages with those you work with in your ministry and make them a topic to discuss when you're next together, planning your Messy Church?

CHAPTER 6

GENERATIONS TOGETHER: IT'S THE WAY FORWARD

Being intentionally all-age in Messy Church

'The trouble is that what you're suggesting is simply unrealistic and unworkable!'

This is not an uncommon reaction whenever the idea of intergenerational church is proposed. Strong feelings can often be aroused within congregations that are considering running an all-age service, even if only once a month. Decades, arguably centuries, of doing things in separated groups make it very difficult for many people even to consider another way of being church. Even when it is argued that there are other times during the month when it's possible to do 'traditional church' with a like-minded group, and that the one time in the week when we can all be together should by default be intergenerational, many remain unconvinced. It's not that they are being deliberately obstructive: there is a genuine feeling that church works best when we recognise that the mysteries of our faith need to be approached in different ways and with different levels of understanding for different groups that make up the body of Christ.

One argument goes like this: children are developmentally at a different place from adults, so church needs to be shaped in a language and format that works for them. In a similar vein, adults have particular grown-up interests and issues that cannot be tackled comfortably when children are present, so there needs to be the opportunity for sustained listening to a well-reasoned and well-presented sermon on such themes. Perhaps most importantly, due reverence towards things sacred and the biblical injunction that all things should be done 'decently and in order' confirm the truth that it is just not possible to worship with a wide range of age groups present, with their differing attention spans, interests and abilities. Those who are advocates of intergenerational worship and learning clearly shouldn't brush aside these arguments. They deserve to be addressed.

IT'S NOT ABOUT AGE

Perhaps the first step when tackling these objections is to recognise that many of the frustrations identified as issues in all-age worship have nothing at all to do with age differences. Tastes, preferences and spiritual insights can be found to be equally present or absent within every generational group of a congregation. Recent work on spiritual styles by the Canadian theologian David Csinos has been very helpful in this respect. He identifies four different ways in which people of all ages respond to the presence of God in worship and in the way they wish to express their faith. These are a word-centred, an emotion-centred, a symbol-centred and an action-centred response.[26]

Even without these insights, it is surely obvious that a young child from a Christian family will have more experience of worshipping God than an adult who has just come to church to hear his or her banns read. To take further examples, an enquiring teenager could easily have a deeper biblical understanding of current environmental issues than someone who has worshipped at the same church their whole life long but has never thought about such things, and a mature grandparent often finds more delight in listening to and working with young children than those of normal parenting age. We do a great injustice to any age group if we box people into stereotypical categories, suggesting that 'because they're children' they are bound to like busy, frenetic activities and can't do quiet reflection, or, equally, 'because they're old' they will only enjoy traditional hymns and won't like music to be too loud. One of the great joys of my visits around the UK has been to meet people in their 70s, 80s or even 90s who throw themselves with a passion into working with young families and children in Messy Church. Rather than being discomfited by noisy and maybe messy activities, they have expressed delight at being able to sit alongside new spiritual grandchildren in their church and to offer them welcome and friendship.

CHILDREN SHOWING THE WAY

Similarly, I don't believe that all-age worship is an issue about stages of faith. There can be a deep and genuine awareness of God among the youngest in a congregation, and the insights that come 'out of the mouths of babes and infants', as the psalmist tells us (Psalm 8:2, NRSV), can have a spiritual depth and power way beyond what might be expected if we go by an age-related model of spiritual development.

In my experience of Messy Church, it is often the children who lead the way when it comes to asking the questions. I met Natalie on a training day for Messy Church not long ago. When I was explaining that Messy Church is about reaching out in a spirit of mission to the two or three generations who have not been touched by our Christian story in the UK and is therefore largely for those who would never have been to a church before, her reaction was, 'That was me.' She had been invited to Messy Church by a friend and had brought along her family. She had had no previous experience of church at all. She loved the lively, welcoming and creative atmosphere and was delighted to see how much her children also enjoyed being there. 'I got more and more involved and offered to help,' she explained, 'but it was the children who took me to the next level. They were hearing stories about Jesus and that prompted questions from them, questions I didn't know how to answer. This led me to join a Christianity Explored group, where I came to faith myself, and so, together with the whole family, I was baptised.' Natalie has gone on to be part of another team, starting a new Messy Church.

On another occasion, I was sitting down at a Messy Church meal after we had explored a Bible story with activities and a time of celebration. On the table there were some questions to consider as we ate together. Unsurprisingly (this is Britain, after all!) the adults around me weren't particularly interested in talking about faith; it was the children who took up the questions and got us all discussing which part of the Bible story we liked best and which was the most important part for us that day.

The church in recent decades has had a serious rethink about the importance and depth of children's spirituality, and this can have a huge bearing on our understanding of the potential of intergenerational church. If we seriously begin to recognise that children are equal partners with grown-ups in our experience of the kingdom of God, it makes perfect sense that their contributions should be received and valued when we meet together, and we need the opportunity to be truly alongside each other for that to happen. It strikes me that there is a rich possibility for spiritual cross-fertilisation here, which those who advocate separation in ministry are missing. Children often know God but cannot name him, simply because they don't have the religious language in which to express their experiences; whereas adults often know the language but don't necessarily know God. Put the two together and both grow into a richer and deeper faith.

CHILDREN IN THE MIDST

Another area of disquiet concerning all-age worship centres on the fact that it is perceived as having to be child-focused, which can leave those who are single or married without children feeling that church is not really for them. This is a serious and important consideration and, of course, can be extended to many other groups who feel that the language at church, the content of the services and even sometimes the pronouncements from the pulpit make them feel like outsiders, unwelcome within the church community.

It's important to remind ourselves that those who were most marginalised by their society felt most drawn towards Jesus. He took steps to come alongside the people whom nobody else bothered with. He even reached out and touched them, or allowed them to touch him—and both of these actions brought criticism from the 'outraged' religious leaders of his day. If our all-age worship is excluding groups and making them feel uncomfortable, it is not true intergenerational church.

Having children present does *not* mean that the experience of worship and learning has to be child-focused. Children in the midst shouldn't dictate the agenda but, rather, change the atmosphere. They set the temperature for a congregation to be open to surprises, comfortable with change, ready to wonder and, most importantly, willing to learn new things in a playful way. In this sense, the presence of children reminds us of what is important about our journey of faith alongside each other. As the saying goes, 'We don't stop playing because we grow old; we grow old because we stop playing' (George Bernard Shaw). Surely this is why Jesus took a child and stood him or her in the midst of his disciples to remind them how to enter the kingdom of heaven.

LARGE CONGREGATIONS

One of the more robust objections that I have met, regarding intergenerational worship, is that it's too challenging to do with a large congregation. This has also been an major issue for some Messy Churches, which have found themselves overwhelmed with 150 people or more coming along. Their cry has been that there is no time to make the friendships that are so much at the heart of Messy Church. They are unable to give newcomers proper attention and make them feel welcomed and, most importantly, remembered.

Certainly, there are challenges when numbers grow in any church setting; it becomes more difficult to create the sense of belonging and ownership that is so important for a positive experience of intergenerational worship and learning. It is natural that such large gatherings tend to default to a presentation mode from the front, however interactive they try to make it, and the congregation becomes a group of passive spectators more than active participants in what is happening. This is a challenge for all types of services, whether intergenerational or not, but it is not an argument for dismissing the value and importance of being intergenerational. Large groups require an even greater effort than usual on the hospitality front (hospitality being one of the core values of Messy Church) and churches facing this challenge perhaps need to find a way to break their congregation down into more manageable units where the best of all-age worship can be experienced together.

The advice to many large Messy Churches has been to consider running a second Messy Church at a new time or partnering in some way ecumenically to enable numbers to be managed more sensibly. Having said that, the interactive nature of Messy Church, with its craft tables and freedom of movement, can lend itself far better than many intergenerational models to accommodating larger numbers, as it appeals to so many different learning styles, tastes and attention spans. The fact that the celebration time is kept short in Messy Church is also an advantage in this respect. Perhaps the biggest challenge that most larger Messy Churches face is with the catering, but here again I have come across some ingenious solutions, including, in one Messy Church, a second sitting for the meal.

NOT 'CHURCH LITE'

Intergenerational worship and learning is possible and offers in no way a shallow or superficial experience of worship. Anyone who has worked with children for any length of time will testify that their presence means there will always be plenty of questions raised, which are far from simplistic;

in fact, they are often questions that many adults would like to voice but have never dared ask. Intergenerational worship is not 'church lite', as some would claim, but 'church right'; as I have argued in previous chapters, it captures the true biblical model of one generation coming alongside another, sharing the story of God's love.

FOR REFLECTION

- How open to change are you prepared to be when it comes to trying out a different way of worshipping together?
- What practical and personal difficulties do you foresee for yourself, should you decide to commit yourself to intergenerational church as your regular gathered worship?
- Who is worship for? Do you see worship primarily as a time for you to receive more of the grace of God or are you there to see others blessed?

PART 2

MESSY TOGETHERNESS AND HOW TO DO IT

CHAPTER 7

CREATING TOGETHER

Intergenerational activities in Messy Church

What a privilege it's been to join in with Messy Churches up and down the country over the past years! I have been overwhelmed by hospitality and thoroughly inspired by all the ideas I have picked up on the way. As I have travelled, I have been in listening mode, as it were, aiming to pick up the signs of God at work through Messy Church—and it has been fascinating. Nothing can compare with sitting next to a family, new to church, around a craft table and talking with them about what they enjoyed at Messy Church, what prompted them to come and even what they think it's all about. This sort of 'crafty conversation' is a very special aspect of Messy Church and, of course, is as much part of the experience as anything else planned for that session. Indeed, Messy Church has reminded us all that everything does not hang on the input (or lack of it) in the celebration talk, but rather that journeys of faith start as often amid the paste and paints as anywhere.

ACTIVITIES FOR ALL

Including crafts and physical activities as part of the learning process is nothing new for those who have been involved with children's ministry down the years. What is new in Messy Church is that we offer this hands-on experience of church to adults as well. This is intergenerational craft! Sadly, many grown-ups have left behind their experience of making something for pure enjoyment long ago, probably in primary school. The educational model with which we have worked for the secondary school years has been far too 'serious' and academic to allow much time for experimental play as part of learning. And yet, as recent research has shown again and again, we learn most through play and continue to do so all our lives. G.K. Chesterton once wrote, 'The true object of human life is play. Earth is a task garden. Heaven is a playground.'[27]

How to make the most of your craft tables

It is not always easy to relearn the art of play. Many Messy Church teams will testify that children tend to get stuck into the activity tables quickly, whereas their carers and parents very often hang back as spectators, feeling that it's somehow not for them. It takes an intentional invitation from the table leaders to involve the adults with their children in the process. I have found the following tips to be helpful in making this happen:

- Whoever is leading the craft or activity table needs to be enthusiastic. I suppose that should be obvious, but wherever the table leader clearly delights in what is being made, their joy is infectious. A similar truth applies when telling Bible stories. Unless the storyteller has fallen in love with the story again, no one will want to listen.
- When putting together a craft idea, don't have it all 'done and dusted', with little for people to do apart

from assembling something already cut out, colouring something already designed or following a prescribed set of instructions. I know this sounds daring, but a craft is sometimes far more successful when it is not quite as 'worked out' as we have been schooled to believe it should be. If templates haven't been cut out, don't worry: invite the adults to help with that activity. If instructions are a little complicated, don't worry: invite suggestions from those who are having a go at making the craft. It will certainly increase their ownership and probably even improve the finished product. Be prepared to get a bit more messy than your instincts might at first suggest.

- Don't be constrained by an obsessive desire to make sure a craft looks complete according to the perfect 'one you made earlier'. Sometimes, having a beautiful exemplar can hinder the creativity that the children and adults would like to explore. Invite them to suggest how to improve what you have imperfectly begun. Don't feel you have to keep stepping in and monitoring the creative process to make sure it's on track. The truth is, it's not the finished product that matters; it's the engagement in the creativity that's important. As the craft or activity table leader, you are a significant Christian adult working alongside those who have come along to Messy Church, perhaps for the first time. As such, you are modelling Christ as you work *with* them rather than trying to control the outcome.
- Don't be so possessive about your activity that you are not prepared to let it go. Sometimes, those who come

to Messy Church will have better ideas for the way it should be made or how the game should go. Showing your willingness to listen and receive what they suggest is a way of inviting their ownership of the activity and enabling them to grow in their sense of belonging to Messy Church. I've lost count of the number of times, at my own Messy Church, when I have been surprised and humbled by the way those who have come to the table have added value to what I started. It has helped me move into new learning as the craft activity opens up the story for us both in our Messy togetherness.

- Don't devalue the craft activity 'in your head', because that will soon become apparent in your attitude. Maybe you too are struggling with the idea that this is a good way to learn. Maybe you were brought up to think that sitting still for ages and listening to someone talking is the only way to be taught effectively. Of course, that may be helpful, but it is certainly not the only possible learning style. Kinaesthetic learning, as modelled through the Messy craft time, is vital for us all.
- Another temptation related to the activities and crafts is to go for what is exciting and interesting and almost forget that it needs to tell the Bible story in some way. There are so many good ideas available now that it is all too easy to build your Messy Church around them rather than around the Bible story. Always start with the biblical text and let it shape the sorts of activities that you offer.
- Finally, remember that the time of making and doing things together is part of the teaching and learning

process of Messy Church. It is, in a very real sense, part of the sermon—although that doesn't mean that the table leader needs to give a sermon before groups start making the mosaic cross or decorating their glass jar. Instead, leaders should develop the art of making a simple one-sentence connection with the Bible story of the session. 'Today we're decorating a tree to remind us of the one that Zacchaeus climbed to try to see Jesus'; 'Today we're icing a biscuit with our favourite colours to remind us that God knows about us as individuals and longs to give us good things', and so on. Table cards with one simple open-ended question can also be helpful: 'How long do you think you could last in a desert without food and with very little water?' or 'What helps you to pray?'

Adults and children together

Visitors to Messy Church are often surprised to discover that the whole family is being invited to enjoy what's on offer. You can see the relief and delight in so many parents' faces, not only that they are encouraged to let their children explore the stories through play, but also that they are allowed to be part of it. It's not something happening outside in a separate room, as in traditional church, while the adults sit in pews; nor is it happening in a school classroom, while the parents are out at work. This is about learning together—the adult from the child, as well as the child from the adult. In addition, getting messy at home has been made difficult by our house-proud, materialistic culture. Certainly, as one young mum told me, taking part in all this activity *and* exploring the Bible is 'something my boy just doesn't get anywhere else'.

Keeping a balance in the activities

When it comes to the type of crafts on offer, it has been a delight to witness, on my travels, the unlimited creativity that can be unleashed once teams are open to... well, almost anything. Some of the best crafts, for me, are those that involve doing something just a little bit daring and 'out of the box'—perhaps using tools or electricity, or, in fact, anything that encourages people to be inventive. Just how far, for example, can you catapult a meringue? These more challenging craft activities can draw in parents too, especially dads, and even, on occasion, the glue-and-glitter-averse tweenagers. With so many wonderful ideas out there, in our BRF books, in the *Get Messy!* magazine and on the web (pinterest.com, for example), I can only urge all craft teams to go beyond the rather tame preschool crafts for at least some of the activities you offer: think big, be daring and take a few more risks.

Personally I've got stuck into a lot of different and very creative craft activities during my visits to Messy Churches. However, the best Messy Churches offer a balanced variety that tap into different learning styles.

Here's a creative checklist that might help you review your range of crafts and activities each month. Aim to include as many from this list as your space allows:

- Something crafty and simple
- Something cooperative and large
- Something crafty and complicated
- Something culinary
- Something 'cool' (such as a science experiment)

- Something chaotic and very messy
- Something construction-based
- Something challenging, in the form of a game
- Something that involves colouring and collating
- Something conversational that gets people talking
- Something relaxing (a reflective activity or prayer space)
- Something community-linked (social action or fundraising)
- Something concrete and word-based
- Something cultural, connecting to faith around the world

Perhaps you are surprised to see the inclusion of 'something word-based' in this list. It's a commonly held fallacy that children always prefer active crafts and that those involving lots of words are inappropriate. Children are as different in their learning styles as adults.

Also, a word-based activity doesn't have to be a word-search puzzle. At a Messy Church I visited in the Midlands, where the theme was 'The Lord's Prayer', I was delighted to discover one activity table where Bibles were opened up at Matthew 6 in different versions. The group around the table were busy comparing which versions of the prayer they liked and talking about what each line might mean. At a Messy Church in the north-west, at the time of Advent, one group spent the whole session using letters from two Scrabble sets, creating a crossword that explored all the different names of God, prompted by verses in Isaiah 9.

A few years ago, the BRF Messy Church team put together Messy Church outlines for each of the books of the Bible. At that time, we included a different list of activity types:

- Something for younger participants
- Something for older participants
- Something for girls
- Something for boys
- Something word-based
- Something food-based
- Something that explores a global aspect of faith
- Something that opens up great art
- Something quiet
- Something really messy

Whichever list helps you best, do be encouraged to offer a range of experiences to help people engage with the gospel through Messy Church.

THE IMPORTANCE OF PLAY

The German educator Friedrich Fröbel (1782–1852), known as the 'Father of Kindergarten', felt that young children should not be subjected to formal instruction but should learn through play. In his book *The Education of Man* (first published in 1826), he wrote, 'Play is the highest expression of human development in childhood for it alone is the free expression of what is in a child's soul.'[28] Exploration and play are the real routes to learning the things that matter. Most adults have been 'educated' out of this truth, which is why so many parents at Messy Church are reluctant to let themselves go in order to worship and learn kinaesthetically. Growing up as a Christian isn't just a cerebral process. It needs to involve every part of us—all our senses—so that it might go deep and be truly transformational.

So, never underestimate the importance of the mess in Messy Church! This has been one of my key observations. Church in its traditional forms has struggled with the 'messy' aspect of Messy Church. Too often, craft is tolerated as something for the children, as an attractive way to 'get people in', as merely the warm-up activity for the bit that really matters, rather than a core element of good intergenerational worship and learning. The truth is that it's in the mess that relationships are formed, as old and young, newcomer and team member play together. It's in the mess that our bodies learn the truths, ahead of our minds, and it's in the mess that laughter is released—a vital ingredient and a very special gift of God to the human race, which can enable true worship and learning to take place. Never underplay the play!

FOR REFLECTION

- What is your personal attitude to learning through crafts, activities and games?
- Do you have examples from your own life of how creativity has helped you on your journey of faith?
- What does being made in the likeness of God, who is a creator, mean for you?
- How might you be more creative in your worship and learning? How might you best encourage others to be so, too?

CHAPTER 8

CELEBRATING TOGETHER

Intergenerational Bible storytelling, music and prayer

One observation, above all, has stood out for me as a result of my travels around UK Messy Churches: there is often a real problem when it comes to the 'Messy celebration'. I believe there are two main reasons for this issue.

UNDERSTANDING WORSHIP

First, there is a misconception that the bit that *really* matters at Messy Church happens in the 15–20 minutes given over to Bible story, song and prayer. In other words, if we don't get this 'worship moment' right, the rest of the Messy Church activities have been in vain. This is just not true and it betrays a complete misunderstanding of Messy Church and Messy togetherness.

Perhaps it has something to do with our contemporary use of the word 'worship'. Worship has come to mean a particular time-related activity, usually containing lots of music of whatever tradition, in which there is a strong focus on praising God by individuals who have chosen to do this alongside other individuals. However, this is not a biblical definition of worship. The words 'worship' and 'service' are related to each other in the original Greek of the New

Testament and in the experience of both Jewish and Christian traditions. Our worship is not just that corporate moment involving liturgy, listening and music; it means all our life being given over to serving God. Paul puts it most clearly when he urges his readers, 'Offer your bodies to him as a living sacrifice, pure and pleasing. That's the most sensible way to serve God' (Romans 12:1). Other versions translate the last phrase as 'your acceptable worship'.

In other words, worship is a whole-life response to God, perhaps nurtured and stimulated by what happens when we get together but definitely not confined to that moment in time. We might even say that our true worship begins once the 'service of worship' is over and we leave the building.

The exaltation of liturgical corporate worship means that other worship activities have become devalued. *All of Messy Church is worship* (as is our service of God in the weeks that follow). The activities are part of the worship, as is the meal we share together. If our celebration is viewed as the one 'true' moment of worship, that will have a negative effect on the rest of our Messy Church and will lay expectations on the relatively short time of celebration which it was never designed to bear.

REIMAGINING GATHERED WORSHIP

The other dimension of the problem with the celebration has its roots in the chequered history of all-age worship, as outlined in Chapter 2. Rather than seeing the Messy Church celebration as an opportunity to reimagine intergenerational gathered worship, we have brought to the table a host of inherited mistakes about what works and what doesn't when there are children present. The celebration moment has either become entirely child-focused or it has repeated failed patterns from past models of family worship. Just as with all of Messy Church, we need to do some new thinking when we celebrate in an all-age way. We may be using the traditional material of visual aids, action songs and storytelling, but this should not mislead us into thinking that we are doing it all just for the children's sake.

Our rethinking could start with the allotted time period for this part of Messy Church. Those who have been involved in intergenerational worship on a Sunday morning, and those who come from particular church traditions, are often surprised by the recommended 15 minutes for the celebration slot. Surely, they think, that's no time at all in which to do 'worship' justice and to tell and explain a Bible story adequately to the congregation. It's no wonder, then, that many Messy celebration slots drift beyond the allotted time, and are not successful.

So why does the standard Messy Church template suggest such a relatively short slot for a celebration together? Primarily, there is a clear recognition that, as in other parts of Messy Church, we need to start where people are. Our own experience of church may have conditioned us to the idea that singing songs for a long period of time, or listening to a talk for longer than 10–15 minutes, or being quiet during prayers, is the norm. However, this sort of expectation is not found in many walks of life outside church, and is one of the many things that visitors find strange when they first walk through the doors for a traditional Sunday morning service. Although we might think it would be good for people to focus for longer, experience silence and learn to listen, this is simply not where people are. Messy Church recognises this and works with it rather than presenting yet another barrier to people coming to faith.

Even these 15 minutes of celebration are broken up into three sections. This is the time to gather together all that has been shared and experienced during the activities; this is the time to connect all the activities in with the key Bible story being told; and this is the opportunity for a shared time of prayer and reflection. However, the celebration shouldn't seek to do everything; and, in particular, it should not be used to ram home a message or get people to respond with personal commitment. These things could happen and have happened in Messy Church, but they should not be the overriding agenda of the celebration.

Finally, the presence of children in the celebration, rather than being a challenge (or even, for some, a problem), can turn out to be its greatest strength. This is the miracle of good intergenerational worship and learning. The children's enthusiasm and willingness to participate sets the temperature for the way the celebration should be handled and prevents it from becoming a one-way process with a didactic style of teaching. The involvement of children forces it to become interactive, not just for a few moments before the 'serious message' is shared, or just during the singing. Every aspect of the celebration needs to encourage dialogue and participation. This style of conversational learning, even during the gathered worship, is a vital and significant element in reimagining the way we do faith together in Messy Church.

Perhaps by now you are feeling a little daunted and seriously wondering whether a Messy Church celebration according to these guidelines is truly possible! Let's look at some useful hints about each aspect of the celebration.

SHARING THE BIBLE STORY

It still comes as a shock to many who run Messy Churches that our precious stories from the scriptures, which we may have known since childhood, are brand new to most of the families who come along to Messy Church. Schools workers, however, have known this for a long time. Those who go into community schools in particular, with the opportunity to share a Bible story as part of collective worship or explore aspects of faith in class as part of the RE syllabus, know that it's necessary to start from scratch. We cannot assume that the children will have any understanding of the context of the story or be at all familiar with the religious language that is often part and parcel of those stories.

The significance of the fact that Zacchaeus was a tax collector won't be understood; an understanding of what it means to be a shepherd caring for sheep will be largely absent, especially in our cities; and there will be no knowledge of religious groups such as the Pharisees and scribes. At one Messy Church I visited, we sang a popular church song about being like sheep, which included the words 'Sadducees' and 'hypocrisy'. As I looked around, I noticed the blank faces among many of the families there; indeed, not many of them were singing anyway.

As if for the first time

How do you go about telling Bible stories 'as if for the first time'? My best advice is that, first and foremost, storytellers need to fall in love with the story again and find a way of telling it that conveys their own wonder and enthusiasm for it. They then need to use language that is uncluttered and stripped of inherited religious jargon. The best preparation for telling a Bible story well is to read it again and again… and again. Let it become so much a part of you that you can tell it with a passion that will be caught by all who listen, and certainly without any words in front of you that might get in the way.

One of the keys to that infectious passion is that when you read the story prayerfully and honestly, you ask questions and develop an openness to new discoveries, with even the most familiar of Bible stories. It sometimes helps to ask yourself, 'Which part of the story surprises me this time? Which part of the story makes me angry and fills me with questions? Which part of the story would I like to hear more about than is recorded here in the passage?'

Guidelines for intergenerational storytelling

- Always remember to welcome all the generations present at the beginning and during the celebration.
- Plan to be inclusive with whatever activity, dialogue or presentation you intend to use.
- If you're inviting children up to do something, always invite adults too. This story is for everyone.
- Do not prepare something 'just for the children'. You will almost inevitably run the risk of talking down to them. In fact, children learn mainly not from your words but from the non-verbal dimension of what is happening, so prepare for your adult audience too.
- Plan your presentation as a dialogue, developing your theme through questions and answers.
- Use simple activities, which make the presentation interactive.

- Don't use closed questions (those that can be answered by one word only).
- Don't have one 'right' answer in mind, for which you as the storyteller painfully search, dismissing all the others on the way. Instead, accept and, wherever possible, use all answers. Remember that intergenerational learning is a two-way process.
- Don't keep asking the same people to participate, however eager they may be.
- Don't just work at the front with a small group in a limited area, as the rest of the Messy congregation will quickly feel excluded.
- Do make it fun! Every element doesn't have to have some immediate and deep spiritual connection.
- Celebrate the willingness and involvement of those who take part.
- Keep your examples and illustrations clear, concrete and uncluttered. Any pictures need to be larger than you think, and fonts used for the words need to be very large and bold. Check that everything can be seen from the back of the church. An alternative is to have multiple copies of words or pictures that can be passed around.
- Practise your presentation beforehand. Why not record it on your phone and play it back as you travel somewhere? This will mean that you fix the outline in your head and you won't need to keep referring to notes, which is to be avoided if at all possible.
- Once you have told the Bible story well, have just one clear message you want to share, which is as much for you as for anyone else.

- Tell the Bible story with energy, using movement, facial expressions, eye contact, pauses and changes in volume.
- Use all the senses to convey the message. This will mean providing different entry points for different people in the Messy congregation—through music, actions, emotions, and what they see or smell or even taste.
- Don't be static in one place, but move around. Be part of the learning together.
- Be ready to hear some of the new insights that will come from the Messy congregation, especially from the children. Share your delight in learning something new.
- Include as many thoughtful questions as helpful answers. Use phrases like 'I wonder...' which invite the children and adults to use their imaginations and engage personally with the story.
- Finally, be disciplined about time: keep it crisp. It helps to know the answers to these questions: What is my opening line? What is my closing thought/question? What is my key message?

SINGING A CHRISTIAN SONG

I've lost count of the number of times, on my visits to Messy Churches, when the choice of songs has clearly been governed by what the music group enjoys on a Sunday morning rather than what will make sense to newcomers to faith. We need to recognise that this can be a real problem for many Messy Church teams.

Once again, maybe we are so locked in to our own experience of church, an experience stretching back to childhood for some of us, that we don't realise how strange it is to put deep feelings about faith into words which we then sing out loud in front of everybody. Musical tastes are very varied and, for most people, singing has a very particular context. Perhaps it is associated with being alone in the shower or plugged into a phone, or picking up the challenge of taking part in a karaoke session while out with friends, or perhaps celebrating with others at a sports ground. In fact, the whole idea of singing in a church, even a Messy Church, and doing so alongside others from different age groups, can be so fraught with challenges that some Messy Churches have decided that singing is not at all helpful for them. When we do sing, clearly we need to think very hard about the types of songs we choose.

Advice on choosing a song for Messy Church

- What sort of words are we asking our invited congregation to sing? Are they about a committed, personal and perhaps emotional expression of faith? If so, is it appropriate to ask people to sing words that they do not yet believe?
- What are the words of the song saying about God? Musical tastes may be controversial but there is no doubt that music is a hugely powerful medium, so what sort of understanding of God is being promoted through the songs we are singing together? Is it an honest and faithful representation not just of how much God loves us but also of how much God understands our deepest and most painful thoughts and feelings? Is it so exuberant, or even triumphalistic, that there is no room

for an understanding that God cares about our doubts, fears and questions?

- As in our retelling of the Bible story, are the words easy to comprehend by those who haven't been brought up with the language of faith? What's the point of singing about 'the days of Elijah', for example, with a group of people who have no idea who Elijah was?
- Thinking of the music itself, how easy is it to sing? I write as one who is not particularly musical and needs to be introduced gently to the enjoyment of singing a new Christian chorus, hymn of praise or worship song. On a very practical note, too, the meaning of the words needs to match the way they are displayed on a screen—for example, with the natural pauses coming at the end of each line.
- There are some songs that have been composed for a congregation to sing and others that are far more suited to a specialist group who can interpret the more complex music or phraseology. We need to distinguish between music that's good to listen to and the sort of song that will enhance intergenerational singing. In this context, short songs, call-and-response songs and songs with a simple repeated phrase work best for most of us in Messy togetherness.
- Thinking of the one song chosen (and, most times, just one song is enough), how does it help everyone to understand the whole of the worship that is Messy Church? How is the song related to the theme of the activities and the Bible story, the focus of this particular Messy service and the prayers to come?

Some Messy Churches do struggle to find the right sort of music for the celebration. This has led a few to write music of their own that better suits the context. I have been to Messy Churches that have their own 'Messy song' or where people have written new words to simple recognisable tunes, including nursery rhymes, rather than choose something from the repertoire that is more suited to a Sunday morning gathering of the faithful. It interesting that when there were revivals of Christian mission in the past—for example, during the Methodist movement in the 18th century—these revivals were often accompanied by the creation of new hymns and songs, some of which made use of well-known tunes from the alehouse. As John Wesley observed, 'The devil should not have all the best tunes.'

USING A CHRISTIAN PRAYER

The final element of the celebration is prayer. Interestingly, in my experience, this is the part that often gets left out. Indeed, prayer gets left out of so much of our Christian living, and Messy Churches and their teams need reminding of this as much as any of us. Yet, perhaps to our surprise, this is a part of the celebration that people may understand better than we realise. It can also come very naturally to an intergenerational congregation.

A prayer activity

Some Messy Churches now regularly include a prayer station as one of the activity tables because prayer is something that a lot of people believe in. They may not know to whom they are praying but there is a definite longing in the human spirit to ask for help from someone greater than themselves and to express thanks for something that has blessed their lives. In my own Messy Church, the prayer station is often busy with people who are happy to add their thanksgivings to a prayer tree or write their petitions on a paper prayer flower, which opens when floated on water. Other Messy Churches have prayer request boxes and some have developed a liturgy of lifting the box up and making it a part of the prayer moment in the celebration. Most primary schools encourage 'reflection', which admittedly is a less focused word than 'prayer' but still recognises that all of us welcome a chance to say something quietly in our hearts to whatever understanding of God we may have.

Interactive prayer

Be encouraged always to include prayer in your celebration, but, as with every other part of Messy Church, aim to make it as interactive as possible. Prayer is far more than a moment to close our eyes and listen to some well-chosen words from someone at the front who knows 'how' to pray. We need to create space for all ages to make their own response to whatever they've heard in the story or picked up from a song. However, because long silences can be difficult for some, it is always a good idea to provide something to do which can facilitate reflection and prayer. It may be something to look at, a hand action or whole-body movement that illustrates the words, or even something as dramatic as writing prayers on paper aeroplanes that go flying off around the church for others to pick up and take home.

Some Messy Churches have begun to include a regular, special prayer as part of a liturgy that Messy Church is developing. Of course, the Lord's Prayer belongs in this category and some churches now pray it using sign language. There is the Messy Grace, with actions, as set out in the first *Messy Church* books by Lucy Moore,[29] which is a fun prayer of thanks for the food that people are about to eat. Jane Leadbetter's excellent book *Messy Prayer* is full of brilliant ideas for praying in your celebration.[30]

CONCLUSION

The Messy celebration is not the most important part of Messy Church but of course it does need to be done well. This is a moment to tell a Bible story that may never have been heard before. This is a moment to sing something about God that will stay with the children and adults well beyond the Messy Church gathering once a month. This is the moment to let everyone know that God longs to be in touch, that God loves everyone there and that God promises to listen to all of their cries and offers to put his arms around them and bless them.

FOR REFLECTION

- How do you define worship?
- Because the celebration in Messy Church is for a different 'audience' from that in a more traditional service, do you tend to think that this worship is inferior in some way?
- Think back to a time when you heard a Bible story told with all ages present. What worked and what didn't?
- What do you understand by the description 'children's songs'?
- Which songs do you think work best in a Messy Church celebration? Are they necessarily 'children's songs'?
- What part, if any, might silent prayer have in Messy Church?

CHAPTER 9

EATING TOGETHER

Intergenerational meals in Messy Church

I have eaten more than my fair share of fish fingers, baked potatoes, sandwiches and cakes during my three years of visiting UK Messy Churches! But I certainly wouldn't have gone without any of them.

The Messy Church meal is one of the most distinctive features of Messy Church's expression of intergenerational worship and learning, and, to my mind, one of its most important. Messy meals have not just fed my stomach but have been times when I've talked at length to people attending the Messy Church, hearing their stories, sharing opinions on a wide range of topics in a relaxed way, talking about faith and, of course, making friends. I couldn't have done my work as a Messy Church listener and encourager nearly as well without the opportunities provided by the meal, and no Messy Church can afford to neglect the meal if it is taking its mission seriously.

HIGH AND LOW TEAS

The meal comes in various shapes and sizes, and not all of them are ideally suited to the sort of friendship making and faith sharing that I'm talking about. Many Messy Churches opt for a high tea as their preferred style of eating together, and this choice certainly makes sense for some, especially for afternoon Messy Churches at the weekend. Often, it is driven by the fact that a Messy Church doesn't have cooking facilities or the space to prepare and provide a warm meal.

One Messy Church in south London faced just such a challenge, but I was particularly impressed by their solution. Rather than having sandwiches and cakes set out on a table where people could help themselves, buffet style, the Messy guests were invited after the celebration to sit at tables, with menus from which they could choose drinks. The drinks were brought to them by Messy team members. On each table, there were some plates set out with food, but then, halfway through the meal, splendid cakes were carried in, on tiered cake stands—just like something out of the Ritz. Apparently the cake stands weren't too expensive to buy, but what an impression they made on us all! They made the cakes look even more delicious. This tea was presented to a high standard, making the guests feel special. Eating together around a table made the occasion feel important, which of course it was.

On my travels I have only occasionally come across such memorable high teas; often they have been rather 'low teas' by contrast. An offer of two cakes and a cuppa is hardly different from the tea and biscuits at the end of a traditional Sunday service, and I don't think this can adequately express the Messy Church value of memorable and distinctive hospitality. It suggests that the Messy Church team doesn't yet see quite how important the meal is or can be. We would never think of inviting our friends to our homes for an evening meal without offering them our best food and drink. It's an essential ingredient to help people relax and talk and get to know each other. A cupcake devoured in two mouthfuls or fewer can't possibly provide that kind of opportunity.

THE PARTY MEAL

There have been meals on my visits that have fallen short in other ways, too. One common experiences is to be presented with a 'party meal'—by which I mean that everything on the table is geared solely to the needs of the children (fish finger sandwiches, as one example). Often, as a result, the adults opt out of eating, declaring that they will do so at home later. As you can imagine, it isn't long before the children also opt out of sitting at the table, and all the hoped-for togetherness around the meal evaporates.

Once again, I feel this is a misunderstanding of what it means to have children in the mix in an intergenerational expression of church such as Messy Church. The fact that children are there doesn't mean that everything must be geared to them and their needs. They shouldn't be responsible for forcing everything to a lowest common denominator when it comes to the menu on offer at meal time. Restaurants and cafés in the secular world get it right when they make sure there is 'family friendly' food available, so why can't the church?

THE FAMILY MEAL

It is widely recognised in the Western world that the 'family meal' is an endangered species in most homes nowadays, so Messy Church's inclusion of this element is distinctly countercultural. Most of us, when pressed, have no problem in recognising the huge value of sitting down to eat together; we know how positive an experience it can be, as an intergenerational community learns to listen to as well as share with each other. The truth is that we have simply given in to pressure and convenience, defaulting to the microwave meal on a tray as we sit separately in silence on the sofa in front of the television.

It's not without good reason that most of the major world religions have chosen to pass on the heart of their faith story via some sort of festival meal, where all ages are gathered and all contributions welcome. If we are serious about nurturing faith and growing disciples in Messy Church, the sit-down meal is one of the first places to explore what this means in practice.

THE HOT MEAL

As you can imagine by now, I have been especially disappointed to visit a Messy Church where the meal has simply been left out. I know there can be many pressing and valid reasons for this to happen, but I remain unconvinced. Choosing to omit this part of the experience of Messy Church definitely means that it is diminished for all who come.

I have also come across many Messy Churches that, when faced with the challenge of providing a meal, have found ingenious solutions to the problem. For example, I have enjoyed pizzas that have been bought in; watched a set of six slow-cookers arrive, like the cavalry, just in time to save the day; and, of course, been treated to traditional fish and chips, hot from a local takeaway. There is something really welcoming about being served with hot food. I've heard so many families express sincere appreciation for it that I can't believe it isn't worth trying to find a solution. Hot food certainly warms hearts and opens people up to life-changing conversations in a way that the lone sandwich can never aspire to.

PRACTICALITIES

Having said all this, I do recognise that the meal can be a huge challenge to a Messy Church team. Even when there is someone on board who has a flair for catering, it isn't at all easy. Some Messy Churches are very pressed for space and there can be an interval of near-chaos while tables are hastily cleared of glitter and glue, cleaned and disinfected, and places are set for eating. One response is to go for the buffet-style approach that I mentioned earlier, but this doesn't always prove the best option. It is difficult for people to wander around with food, especially if young children are in the mix. Conversations become snatched between juggling acts as people attempt to hold on to drinks and plates without dropping anything. In addition, children are apt to gather in a special corner of their own and the whole intergenerational nature of the meal breaks down.

The furniture used for Messy Church can also be a challenge. One that I visited took place in a school, where they had decided to serve the meal in the school canteen. Here, there were fixed low seats in groups of four—ideal for processing a primary school in two sittings through the lunch hour, but not so good for enabling families to meet other families as they ate together. In this Messy Church, the team now uses a different pattern. The long table, such as is popularly used in a street party for a special occasion, is ideal for Messy Church meals. Several families can be within talking distance of each other and can be encouraged to share in both the serving and the clearing away of the meal.

THE TEAM JOINING IN

Another interesting aspect of the meal is something that has happened so often on my travels that I feel it's worth mentioning. I can fully understand, especially with small Messy Church teams, that the leaders often feel they need to hang back at mealtime, to make sure that all the guests get a seat and there is enough food to go around, but also because there can be such a lot of other things to do. However, I always find it sad when this happens, because the meal is such a significant opportunity for relaxed friendship making between team members and the people who are becoming regular visitors or, as is always the case for some at Messy Church, are there for the first time. This is our big faith-sharing moment, every bit as important as the celebration or the discussions at the activity tables.

It may seem like organisational suicide, but I'm sure it would be so much better if the team sat down and ate with everyone else, leaving the tidying up for later. After all, this is *Messy* Church and there are more important things than stacking chairs, folding tables and starting the washing-up, especially if it's at the expense of making the guests feel welcomed.

A SACRAMENTAL MEAL

In a traditional church service, we are no strangers to the idea of having a sacramental meal as part of our worship. The breaking of bread and drinking of wine as part of the Eucharist or Holy Communion is one of the ways in which we express our shared togetherness as Christians in the body of Christ. Eating and drinking together in table fellowship is such a vital part of the way our faith is nourished.

I think we can also apply the term 'sacramental' (in other words, 'that which has a specialness about it', that signposts God's presence among us) to the mealtimes in Messy Church. In fact, there are some Messy Churches that include the sharing of bread and wine before the traditional meal. It was in the context of a shared meal that the first Christians included the service of bread and wine, and there are surely some important parallels to explore here. Today's Messy Churches can grow into a eucharistic community simply because the people have already got used to eating together.

If we began to move towards an understanding of the Messy meal as sacramental, I think it would help us all to see the unmissable value of this part of Messy Church. It is a soul-satisfying moment as much as a stomach-filling one. Some Messy Churches include questions to talk about at the table or offer an opportunity to write down things that they would like the church on Sunday morning to pray for. Jane Leadbetter, a member of the BRF Messy Church team, encourages people to write, on the paper tablecloths, their responses and thoughts about that day's Messy Church. The meal offers a chance to celebrate birthdays, share news and look forward to the next time everyone will be together. Some Messy Churches say the Grace together at this moment, in order to finish well.

TOP TIPS FOR AN INTERGENERATIONAL MEAL

Drawing together some of the key points in this chapter, here are a few guidelines for how best to handle the Messy Church meal.

- Whatever sort of meal you decide to offer, make sure it's the very best you can do.
- If at all possible, offer a hot meal. It's so much more inviting and memorable.
- Let your meal and the way you present it say something about the generosity of God's love.
- Purchase a few high chairs so that families with babies feel welcomed.
- Don't let the children eat together on a special table with small chairs, set apart from the rest.
- Encourage families to sit down together with other families.
- Lead by example as a team by joining everyone at the tables.
- End well. Use the meal as your final gathered moment to celebrate special events, share prayer needs, advertise forthcoming events and give out 'take-home sheets' or special gifts after the day's Messy Church

GOSPEL MEALS

Sharing food together was the context for much of Jesus' ministry in the Gospels. His table talk and the stories he shared between courses are well documented, and this clearly demonstrates how faith and food can go hand in hand. It is still the tradition in most parts of the world to express hospitality by the provision of a proper meal, and in this respect Messy Church is only repeating a lesson in welcome and evangelism whose value is well attested. The shared meal is a central ingredient in successful intergenerational worship and learning. It is the place where so much vital Messy conversation happens, so please, do not allow it to drop off your Messy Church menu.

FOR REFLECTION

- How much does your Messy Church team or Sunday congregation value the idea of sitting and eating together as part of the gathered worship?
- What ingenious solutions have you found for providing hot food?
- What do you think about the idea of including the sharing of bread and wine as part of a church meal together?

CHAPTER 10

WORKING TOGETHER

Intergenerational teams in Messy Church

Today I met young Amy, who is in Year 5 at primary school. She was in charge of one of the table activities, as well as being an active member of the worship band. The singing was led by older teenagers and a young mum, who later told me that she was taking her first steps back to faith. Two of the Messy families brought up the special Messy Church collection boxes—two large and gaudily painted piggy banks, in the shape of a pig and a sheep. Everyone is encouraged to make a small contribution, noisily, into either of these boxes, and they are brought up as part of the celebration.

This extract is taken from a reflection I wrote after one of my Messy visits and it illustrates something that I am discovering in many Messy Churches. The very nature of the way things are structured within Messy Church gives plenty of opportunity for whole-congregation involvement. The youngest to the oldest can have a part to play, whether they are on the planning team or not. This isn't how church has been done traditionally, where too often a small, ordained or trained leadership conducts the service from the front, while the congregation sit or stand—sometimes their only participation in what is going on. Messy Church is about shared ownership of all that happens and, most importantly, this involves the generations working alongside each other.

LAY LAY LEADERSHIP

It has come as a surprise to some within traditional church denominations that many fresh expressions of church are largely led by lay people. This is particularly true of Messy Church. However, here it is not even simply about leadership by non-ordained members of the congregation who have nevertheless received some training; Messy Church is, more often than not, led by 'lay lay leaders', a term coined in the Church Army research into UK fresh expressions of church entitled *From Anecdote to Evidence* (2014).[31]

Of course, many people from non-liturgical and non-denominational church traditions have always understood that Christian worship and learning are the responsibility of the whole congregation. The professionalisation of highly trained leaders can often lead to a disabling of the rest of the congregation and be a blockage to the exercise of their spiritual gifts for the building up of the body of Christ, as Paul describes it in Ephesians 4:11–16. The importance of 'every-member ministry' is being rediscovered in many churches, of course; even so, there can be understandable tensions when some still strongly advocate the particular ministry of 'priest' as ordained leader, and leave others feeling relegated to a second-class ministry. For example, many of us involved in children's ministry often feel that our work in church is not quite as highly valued as the work of those who teach and lead up front in services; the truth is that our ministry and service are every bit as vital to a church as any other calling.

EVERY MESSY MEMBER IS VALUABLE

Messy Church has given us the opportunity to rebalance this thinking about leadership. A primary school child has a role in running a session, just as much as the 'official' ordained leader who chairs the planning group; a young mum who is slowly finding her way back to faith is as important a member of the team as someone with years of mature Christian service behind them. Each has a gift to offer and gifts to receive when they get involved with their local Messy Church.

This is not to say that biblical training and a longer experience of what it means to be a Christian don't matter; of course these things are vital parts of the whole, but they are not the only way to measure the significance of an individual's contribution. There are more than enough examples in the Bible of the life-changing difference made to a situation when a young child stepped up to the mark with his or her faith, or when an adult outsider offered insights into a situation. Naaman's servant girl comes to mind (2 Kings 5), as well as the Syrophoenician mother in her conversation with Jesus (Mark 7:24–30), for example. The messy mix of generations in Messy Church, alongside those not yet with faith, can make this sort of shared inspiration possible.

TWEENAGERS AND TEENAGERS

Having said this, I don't think it's always easy for many of those who run Messy Churches to be open to shared leadership. Our inherited thinking about who should lead and how to lead still shapes much of what goes on, so it is not surprising that the BRF Messy Church team has had to work hard both to discover good examples of intergenerational leadership and to find ways of encouraging it among the Messy network. In order to facilitate this, we were joined for a year by a Messy Church paid intern whose role was to look into the part played by teenagers in Messy Churches around the UK. James Pegg did some valuable research for us, visiting Messy Churches and writing up stories of best practice in this area.

There is no doubt that, in recent Christian history, we have not had a good record of retaining our young people once they make the move into secondary school. There are many reasons for this, of course, but chief among them has been the fact that young people have not always been given a voice and a way of participating in the way we do church together. Some church traditions have been able to offer the opportunity to join a choir or worship band, or maybe to act as servers or on the sound desk; on the whole, however, young people have not felt that church is interested in the gifts they have to offer.

This is at odds with the way things are in the secular world, where society has changed its attitudes in the world of education. For example, many of you will know that children in primary school are encouraged to take on all sorts of responsibilities and leadership positions, on the school council, as part of buddying schemes looking after younger children, or even making decisions about school budgets regarding environmental issues and social events. They are given a voice that they do not often find at church.

BEWARE GENERATIONAL FRAGMENTATION

One of the disappointments most often expressed to me by Messy Church leaders, on my travels, is that the children (and, therefore, their families) do not stay beyond a certain age. The reasons for this can be complex. Often (and this is a hard thing to say), it is because the Messy Church leaders haven't grasped that they are running an all-age expression of church, which needs to be rigorously worked out in the range of crafts on offer, the type of meals served and the way in which the celebration is conducted. However, there are also issues about whether the leadership team is genuinely open to including young people and their ideas, as well as offers of help from new Messy Church families who attend or other members of the congregation who may feel they cannot attend Messy Church unless they have a job to do. Messy Church leaders need to be willing to let go and take even more risks in their Messy mission.

In the early days of Messy Church, there was often a frisson of horror when, at gatherings of Messy Churches, people asked whether it was OK to have non-Christians on the leadership team. I am pleased to say that this has changed over time, and I believe it is a reflection of the growing openness of Messy Churches to show hospitality to those who come, in every way possible—including receiving their help rather than sticking to a policy of working only with those who are part of the 'in-crowd'. We have only to look at the range of people that Jesus himself chose for his leadership team to see the justification for this openness. The Twelve certainly weren't all unshakeable followers and reliable partners in mission, and their agendas were definitely very mixed. Yet Jesus chose them because he saw who they could become rather than who they already were. Messy Church teams need to be similarly inclusive, remembering that the faith-sharing at a Messy Church can happen as much within the team as it does among those who attend.

TAKING A LEAD FROM THE EDUCATIONAL WORLD

For this reason I often encourage teams to be adventurous about who they include among their helpers. Taking a lead from the educational world, we should start to invite upper primary school children to help at each activity table or take part in the celebration. Picking up on the research done for us by James, we need to find ways to include teenagers, with their ideas and passions as well as their unpredictability, in our planning for a Messy Church session. Teams should be alert to offers of help that come from newcomers, too, rather than closing down the offer because 'they won't know where things go' or 'how things are done properly'. Sadly, I have come across just that sort of response.

GUIDELINES

In relation to including older primary school children and teenagers, James drew up a useful set of top tips for making sure a Messy Church works together intergenerationally. Based on his advice, here are some useful guidelines.

- Make connections with the children's and youth groups at your church and invite them to take on a specific role within your Messy Church. These groups may include the uniformed organisations, which often welcome the opportunity to encourage their members to earn a faith or community service badge through their involvement at Messy Church. If you have them, it is also helpful to work creatively with the children's or youth work leaders at your church, seeing it as an opportunity to put faith into action for those in their care.

- When you invite older children and young people to be involved, be prepared to listen to their ideas and give them their head. Things might not always turn out just as you had hoped, but it is far better that they own and run the activity or the song they have suggested than for you to impose what you think would be best.
- Look on the involvement of children and young people in your Messy Church as an opportunity for walking alongside them in their Christian faith development. All of us need encouragement to keep on believing, and this means taking on the role of a mentor to those who join the team. Mentoring isn't all one way though. Be ready to learn something new about your faith from a different generation, whether older or younger.
- Be prepared to extend the range of some of the activities you offer so that they truly reflect the interests and learning styles of the different generations on your team. Challenges, big build activities, quiet games or opportunities just to chill and chat suit some age groups better than others.
- As far as possible, pair up the different generations for particular tasks. Maybe someone older and someone younger could work together at the reception desk or in the kitchen. Sometimes the age groups do prefer to stay together, of course, but be alert to the dangers of too much separation within the all-age mix of Messy Church. Teams need to model the benefits of working intergenerationally so that this will be picked up by the family groups who come along.

- Keep in contact with the children and young people who offer to help from time to time. They won't always be able to get involved—we often underestimate the pressures of school work and exams, for example—so, using social media and other relevant communication channels, let them know that they are valued and that they are always welcome. Working intergenerationally means looking out for each other beyond our own comfortable peer groups.

INTERGENERATIONAL MISSION

Intergenerational mission teams can be particularly effective. Not only are they training opportunities within themselves, allowing wisdom and experience to be passed between the generations, but they also model the way that faith is best caught and nurtured. It seems that such teams were probably part of the New Testament experience among the first Christians. Paul gathered his various apprentices around him on his missionary journeys and he acted as a spiritual father to some of them, especially to Timothy. When Paul and Barnabas first left Antioch to take the gospel to Cyprus, they took with them John Mark, who was a younger cousin to Barnabas. Although this relationship did not work out too well, at least they took the risk of including Mark. Later Barnabas went back to Cyprus with Mark, where they worked intergenerationally to establish a church on the island. Touchingly, many years later, Paul asked for Mark to join him in Rome because 'he can be very helpful' (2 Timothy 4:11).

On a Messy Church team, there is room for a wide range of creative partnerships between the generations. This means that Messy Church is far more than just a proven way to welcome new families on to a journey of faith. Messy Church is also a faith-growing opportunity for those who get involved and, most importantly, a chance for those who join the team to see how faith is real and active in the lives of a variety of people, not just among those of their own age group. My observation from my Messy Church visits is that the teams who have grasped this intergenerational dimension are more successful at attracting and keeping families who bring along their grandparents, carers, children and teenage siblings. Messy teams need to model the mission and discipleship in which they are engaged.

FOR REFLECTION

- What has been your experience of working in an intergenerational team (at a holiday club or church open day, for example)?
- What part does risk-taking play in working with people from a wide range of ages and with differing levels of commitment?
- Has your church considered setting up some sort of mentoring scheme that links up people from across the generations?
- Have you personally ever benefited from some form of mentoring on your faith journey?
- The Australian theologian Beth Barnett has coined the term 'alongsiding' to describe what is happening when Christians commit to each other as co-mentors. How might this relate to what is happening in Messy Church leadership teams?

CHAPTER 11

DISCIPLING TOGETHER

Intergenerational faith nurture in Messy Church

There is no doubt that Messy Church has got people asking some very fundamental questions about how we have always done church. Not only is it challenging us to rethink the best way to do children's ministry, engage with teenagers and value the spirituality of older people; it is also tackling the big question about how we become committed disciples of Jesus Christ. If Messy Church is church, as its name suggests, can it be a place not only where faith is introduced to people for the first time but also where those who become Christians can develop their faith and bring it to maturity?

This important issue is still a huge stumbling block for many people. At our Messy training sessions around the country, we hear them asking the same questions. Surely Messy Church is just a first step? Surely Messy Church needs something more if we are to see people become true disciples? Surely we can't expect people to grow in their faith where all ages are present and (according to the critics) where 'the meat' of our Christian faith will necessarily have to remain as 'milk'? In other words, is Messy Church capable of making disciples? If it isn't, this adventure in intergenerational church is going nowhere and, at some stage, we will need to transfer to a separate model in order to nurture people's growing faith adequately.

IS MESSY CHURCH ONLY A TOOL FOR EVANGELISM?

To be honest, after more than ten years of Messy Church experience in the UK, we are only just beginning to see some possible answers to these important questions. There is no doubting that the initial enthusiasm for Messy Church has been focused largely on the fact that many thousands of people who have never been to church before are now attending Christian worship. Much previous hostility or apathy towards the Christian faith has been eroded by the cheerful, hospitable and relevant experience of faith offered via the Messy Church format. Messy Church has created a safe meeting place for those who do have faith to come alongside those who have not yet made any commitment to belief in God and in Jesus.

As a tool for mission and outreach, there is no doubting Messy Church's credentials, but is that as far as it can go? Can Messy Church offer more than this? Is Messy Church a place where people can encounter God for themselves and make a commitment of faith that will last? Is it possible to proclaim and nurture the faith at the same time?

Many of these questions are as relevant to our inherited churches as they are to any fresh expression, including Messy Church. It's quite possible for people to attend traditional church services all their life but never take their faith beyond a very elementary first step. Our record of discipling in inherited church is not particularly successful; only in more recent decades have various discipleship courses become popular and successful at taking people on from those first steps into a lifelong commitment to following Jesus. So does that mean that in Messy Church, too, we will have to take people away from their first starting place to some new place of faith nurture, in order for them to become disciples? And what if those other places are not intergenerational but are gatherings of like-aged and even like-minded people?

THE SPECIAL MIX OF MESSY CHURCH

From the outset, it is important to remember that Messy Church was never conceived as a 'first step' to something else. All churches always have a mixture of people at different stages of faith, and this is certainly true of Messy Church. But the fact that there are people of faith alongside those who don't yet believe, far from making the task of Christian nurture more difficult, can make a positive contribution to discipleship. Faith in Messy Church is always being shared, explored and tested in the real world. The 'outsiders', as it were—those with real doubts and questions—are a constant reminder to us to think more carefully through what we believe and why we believe it.

The presence of children is also important in the same way. Far from making it less possible to grow as Christians, the fact that children are there, with their innate spirituality, their surprising insights and their penetrating questions, means that faith grows in a friendly fiery furnace rather than at a separate cosy fireside somewhere else, where the same doubts and questions have to be introduced artificially. As we explored in the first part of this book, faith caught and grown in an intergenerational environment is much more likely to withstand the rigorous shaking of real life as we grow older, simply because we have learned that faith alongside others who have kept the faith throughout all stages of their lives. Children are alongside teenagers who still believe; young adults are alongside children who believe; teenagers are alongside grandparents who still believe, and so on. This is intergenerational discipleship.

MESSY CHURCH DISCIPLESHIP

There are now a number of stories coming from the Messy Church network of just this sort of discipleship happening. There may not be as many as we would like or as many as some people are demanding, but there are reasons for this, I believe. The discipleship journey of people coming to the faith for the first time in Messy Church is much longer than it has been in previous generations. In the past, we have been able to build on the remnants of our Judeo-Christian heritage, which gave us at least some foundations for a living faith. In the UK today and, increasingly, in many places in the Western world, this foundation has crumbled. There are people in Britain who have never been to a church in their lives and have never heard a Gospel story—and they include not just the present generation of children but also their parents and, in many cases, their grandparents too. We are two or three generations removed from our Christian heritage, so there is a lot of catching up to do.

There are very few, if any, universally known Bible stories and those who lead the celebration time in Messy Church need to be aware that they will often be sharing something that the congregation is hearing for the very first time. At one Messy Church I visited, where the parable of the lost sheep was told, my conversations with some of the adults afterwards made it clear that they had never heard the story before.

Family discipleship

Another distinctive dimension to Messy Church discipleship is that we are inviting families, not just individuals, on to a discipleship journey. This isn't a new idea; it recalls an earlier time in the church when whole family groups, such as that of the Philippian jailer in Acts 16:25–34, made a commitment together rather than making separate individual responses to Jesus. In Messy Church we often see this happen, and it is the children who lead the way. They enjoy Messy Church and bring home their questions as they hear more about God's love in Jesus. This draws the parents further in and they want to know more because it is all new to them. Not uncommonly, this leads to a baptism in which the whole family witness to their new commitment, not just the child or the adult on his or her own.

Other influences on Messy discipleship

In addition, the frequency of Messy Church meetings—usually just once a month—has an effect on discipleship. There is little dispute over the fact that most adults and children who have never been to church before come to faith through friendships with others who are already Christians. Making friends takes time, and a monthly-only meeting can arguably slow that process down. Sadly, there is also another factor that influences the journey of friendship-making discipleship. Many people in the UK are very suspicious of those who attend church. The church does not enjoy a good reputation, for a number of reasons. It has been damaged by charges of hypocrisy and the scandal of child abuse, for example. Gaining people's trust again, even within the safe environment of Messy Church, can take a long time.

A FARMING ANALOGY

In the parable of the sower, Jesus gives us encouragement as well as sounding a note of realism about people's responses to the good news of the kingdom of God. Lots of things will prevent the seed from either taking root or growing into a successful plant. In this story, only one quarter of the seeds sown bear fruit. The sowing analogy can also help us see that the discipleship challenge, certainly in the UK, goes even further back than simply sowing the seeds. Before that can happen, the land needs to be cleared of stones and then ploughed. Only then can a seed be sown, followed by a long period of waiting, watering and trusting for the right weather conditions, as well as some judicious weeding by the farmer. The journey towards having fields 'white unto harvest' is long.

If we take this picture and imagine what it could mean in terms of people coming to faith, it might look like this:

- Stones are removed: finding that church can be fun
- Land is ploughed: beginning to perceive Christians as OK
- Seed is sown: recognising that 'God stuff' isn't necessarily boring
- There is a waiting time: understanding that God is real, at least to the people who are already Christians
- Seeds are watered: seeing that Jesus is important to these people
- Weeds are removed: admitting that the Bible and Jesus' stories do make some sense

- Soil is warmed: wanting to know a bit more
- First shoots appear: wanting to be part of the faith community

This sort of spiritual mapping of the individual's or family's journey to faith has been researched and expressed in different ways (more details can be found in the book *Making Disciples in Messy Church*).[32] Of course, things can be different. There will be those in whose lives God has already been working long before they turn up at Messy Church, and they could well fall into faith much more quickly than others. On the whole, though, given the spiritual climate within which we are working in the UK, a longer and more prayerful experience of evangelism and discipleship is required in Messy Church.

MESSY EXTRAS

This still leaves the question of whether or not it is better for people to move on to something else, to aid the process of discipleship. Admittedly, we are still in a time of experiment. Some teams, while continuing with their monthly Messy Churches, have gradually begun to introduce 'Messy extras' for families who have begun to show an interest in finding out more and exploring what it means to be a Christian.

In my conversations with Messy Church leaders, however, I have heard that these 'extras' can be quite difficult to get going. One of the main reasons for this is that, in the main, people prefer to stay in Messy Church: it's there that they enjoy being together as a family, with others. The idea of coming along to something different at another time, and perhaps not with the family, is not always welcomed. I met one Messy Church leader who had judged that it was 'the right moment' to invite some mums to come along to an Alpha course to explore faith together with others. However, what happened was that this simply turned them off Messy Church altogether and they have never been seen since. At another Messy Church I visited, one of the table leaders had indeed been on an Alpha course and come back to a living faith of her own, but she still did not want to attend Sunday church. She preferred to return to Messy Church, where she felt most at home. It's not surprising, then, that Messy Church leaders have been very cautious about the type of Messy extra, if any, to introduce.

MESSY DEEPENING

In any case, if Messy Church is church, as we keep insisting, why can't there be a way of taking people further within the parameters of the Messy Church itself? This was crystallised for me after a visit to a Messy Church in the Midlands where the question of discipleship was being seriously addressed. We came to a simple but significant mathematical conclusion. Rather than introducing 'add-ons' or 'take-aways', and rather than 'dividing up' the Messy congregation for discipleship, instead it should be all about the 'times' that we are together! In other words, the key to journeys into faith in Messy Church lies in a *multiplication* of what is already happening rather than the 'take-away', 'add-on' or 'divide-up' model that informs traditional discipleship.

In practice, it could involve any or all of the following:

- Always including a prayer zone as one of the activities.
- Creating opportunities for sharing prayer needs during the meal.

- Widening the range of crafts and activities to include more that are attractive to people with word-based learning preferences.
- Allowing the activities to be more open-ended, rather than having everything prepared in advance.
- Introducing regular simple liturgical elements such as the Lord's Prayer, a simple question-and-answer creed, and the Grace at the end of the meeting.
- Using a regular meal-time grace.
- Introducing 'table talk' as an activity or during the meal.
- Including a zone where people can come together and help prepare something for the celebration—maybe a dance or simple drama, some freeze-frame photos from the story, or a piece of music or poetry.
- Having a question box available, and then addressing some of the questions from time to time as part of the celebration.
- Including an opportunity for someone briefly to share their story of faith.
- Holding a Messy baptism, as part of the celebration, which invites everyone to make a commitment, wherever they are on their journey of faith.
- Including the Eucharist or Holy Communion as part of the celebration and just before the meal.
- Extending your team to include some who act as networkers—not getting involved in any of the activities, celebration or meal preparation, but being

available as a listening ear for those who have questions about faith.

A VARIETY OF DISCIPLESHIP ROUTES

There is clearly no one-size-fits-all shape of discipleship for any church situation, least of all for Messy Church. In fact, the creative approach of Messy Church should encourage us to be creative in the area of discipleship as well. Some people may keep asking questions as their way in to faith, while others come to believe as they get involved more and more with helping to run activities. Some of us like to jump straight in at the deep end, whereas the majority prefer to paddle gently into deeper water.

Gradually deepening what is on offer in Messy Church needs a lot of prayerful thought and creativity, of course. However, I believe that this is the way forward, alongside some of the other creative 'Messy extras', giving us a number of routes to a deeper faith for those who come. As I write, a number of Messy Churches have been running special Messy weekends for their regular congregation. For some, it is just a whole day together in the outdoors, ending with a campfire; for others, it is more adventurous, involving an overnight stay under canvas. The stories coming in from these Messy outdoor activities are encouraging: clearly they have enabled the families involved to take significant steps in discipleship.

For some people, getting involved in acts of service is the real turning point for faith. One Messy Church on the Channel Islands has become well known for taking its team out into local care homes, to offer a taste of Messy Church to the residents. Working together as a Messy Church, young and old in partnership and at different stages of faith, has not only proved to be a blessing to the people they visit but has clearly taken the team on in their faith. Looking back on my own faith journey, I recognise that some of my most significant steps forward in faith were linked to times when I had the opportunity to be involved in a holiday club team, to visit the elderly or sick, or to help plan a special event at a church.

WHAT IS DISCIPLESHIP?

The word 'discipleship' is an important one, with a far wider range of meanings than perhaps we have yet explored. Clearly it is about becoming a learner and a follower, but it's also about being in relationship, just as Jesus was with his first twelve disciples. It's about learning not just from didactic teaching but from being alongside people who model discipleship. It is a community experience not just an individual's response to Jesus. Paul Moore reminds us that, in biblical times, 'belief and behaviour were nurtured with all generations together at both festival and family level'.[33] Messy Church provides a forum for just this sort of shared intergenerational learning from each other. Formal learning is important, of course, but most things of lasting value are picked up as we copy one another and learn by doing. In this sense, discipleship is closely linked to the idea of apprenticeship, where young apprentices learn their trade from the master, who models what to do and then encourages the apprentices to do it themselves.

Blessing, belonging and believing

It is now widely accepted in Christian missional thinking that believing is something that happens after a sense of belonging. This is considered a modern idea, but surely we can find it in the New Testament. People were drawn to the Christian faith because of the remarkably different lifestyle that the first 'followers of the Way' demonstrated: they shared their goods, they cared for their sick and they gave generously to those in need. Belonging to such a group was attractive, especially if you were among those who were being blessed by this overwhelming generosity. As people belonged, they then came to believe—first, no doubt, just with their lips, but soon in their hearts as well, as they discovered the truth of the resurrection of Jesus for themselves and welcomed the presence of the Holy Spirit at work in this new community.

In turn, their beliefs slowly affected their behaviour. We know from Paul's first letter to the Corinthians that there were all sorts of problems in 'messy Corinth'. People had different views on what was right and wrong concerning meat offered to idols, or what was acceptable in terms of marriage relationships, but, as they both belonged and believed, so their behaviour was challenged and transformed. I dare to suggest that this picture of messy Corinth has a lot more in common with many Messy Churches than we might think. Messy Church starts by blessing people with its generosity and warm welcome, which draws people to feel that they want to belong. Within this safe belonging, as people make friends as well as ask questions, they come to believe for themselves. In time, this will affect their behaviour as the Holy Spirit reveals what is not yet quite in tune with the best they can be as sons and daughters of God.

Discipleship isn't some sort of higher degree course for the few who are more fanatical about their faith; it is a gradual process of living more and more like Jesus in the ordinary, everyday things that happen to us. We become disciples together as the generations rub shoulders with each other in the all-age mix of Messy Church.

FOR REFLECTION

- What has been your experience of Christian discipleship?
- What have been some of the most significant learning moments on your faith journey and how did they come about?
- Are there some Christian truths that we can only learn on our own, or do we always need others to help us grow our faith?
- What sort of things can we learn only in community?
- Where and how is discipleship happening at your church?

CHAPTER 12

THE FUTURE IS INTERGENERATIONAL

The prophetic voice of Messy togetherness

The undisputed popularity and success of Messy Church in the UK and in the wider Western world is, I believe, prophetic. Messy Church is not just a theoretical, academic argument for the importance of working intergenerationally but is a living expression of how a church can work out these ideas in practice. It offers us a model for all-age mission and ministry that is working. We cannot claim that it is a perfect model, of course, or that it is without its challenges. Just as you will never find the perfect church, you will never come across a Messy Church that couldn't do things better in some way. The BRF Messy Church team regularly hears from leaders who are quite open about things that are going wrong and about their longing to find a better way forward. However, this is surely a sign of a healthy church movement, not something with which to discredit it. One of the important qualities of the Messy Churches I have encountered has been a humble willingness to listen and an openness to change, prompted by their passion to share God's love with their local communities. These Messy Church teams, while stepping out in faith, are often all too conscious of their own weaknesses and vulnerability as they strive to respond creatively to the great commission to 'make disciples... baptising them in the name of the Father and of the Son and of the Holy Spirit' (Matthew 28:19, NIV).

Many of these pioneers started their Messy Church adventure simply because there were hardly any families with children coming to their normal church services. They hoped that Messy Church would begin to make a difference to their Sunday congregations, but, to their surprise, they discovered that they had embarked on a much bigger enterprise. Slowly they have begun to see that they are a part of something much greater than an attempt to refill empty pews within inherited church. Instead they have stumbled into a new way of being church that can reconnect the generations, so that faith can once again be passed on within the church community and in homes. For many Messy Church leaders, this prophetic dimension of Messy Church is something they have encountered almost by accident, but they are now increasingly embracing it as the way forward for church.

Our inherited model of passing on faith through age-group learning and Sunday-centred teaching has not guaranteed that the coming generation will find faith for themselves. This is not to say that there is no value in continuing with Sunday schools, holiday clubs, adult sermons or peer group discipleship courses. Of course there must still be a place for this approach, but our revived understanding of how faith is best caught and nurtured in an intergenerational context, and the fact that this is happening in Messy Church, is a prophetic reminder to the church that there is another way to ensure that the next generation put their faith in God. An intergenerational way of doing church offers an important balance and corrective to an over-reliance on separate children's, youth and adult ministry, but at the moment it is still largely countercultural for the church in the West. For this reason, it still needs to be championed vigorously—which is why I would dare to say that the future is Messy togetherness. There are several key reasons for claiming this.

THE COMMUNITY FACTOR

Over the last few generations in the West, the individual has become more and more isolated. Many of us who have travelled to countries in the developing world will recognise how community-based their cultures can be, and the extent to which we have lost this element in the way we live. For example, in the UK, older people can go for weeks without seeing another person, and may even die at home and not be discovered for a long time.

I recently met a family friend who had just come back from working overseas as a doctor. She described how, on her return to Britain, she had had to get out of the habit of stopping to talk with everyone she met as she walked along the road—something that was natural in the cities and towns where she had worked. As we have become increasingly aware of this painful difference between cultures, I believe we have awakened a longing to restore a sense of community. At first it was just cosmetic, with the buzzword 'community' simply attached to anything from policing to care, from centres to halls. Genuine community, where people of different backgrounds can meet together and share their common humanity, is not as easy to create as it may seem on paper. I was very impressed by one visit I made to a Messy Church that had started on a big housing estate. It was exciting to hear of the high regard in which it was already held by the local authorities, who are now even prepared to back it with money, because, in their own words, 'This is the best thing happening in this needy community.' Messy Church is among a number of fresh expressions of church that are building on the human need for true community.

THE GRANDPARENT FACTOR

Our Western society is changing, and one of the biggest changes is to do with patterns of family life, including when people get married (if indeed they do) and when and if they decide to have children. Among social groupings where both partners have fulfilling careers for which they have trained, it is not uncommon for them to delay having children until their late 30s or even 40s. Understandably, they may both wish to continue with their work, and this often brings in the 'grandparent factor'. Many people of grandparent age, who may have retired, now find themselves busier than ever, engaged in grandchild-care for part of the week at least, as well as looking after their own even older parents. This particular phenomenon of family life today is bringing the generations together. In some communities that are less affluent, the same thing happens, but it is driven by the need to support each other when money is tight or affordable housing is difficult to find.

In both cases, the generations are reconnecting, whether because of financial pressures or deliberate life choices. Churches need to recognise this trend and offer opportunities for old and young to integrate, discovering how to be together in a creative way. Once again, Messy Church and other similar fresh expressions of all-age worship and learning are meeting the need of the moment.

THE STATISTICS FACTOR

We live in an age of research, which is producing a mesmerising welter of statistical findings about all aspects of life—including church as well as our health and education. There have been a number of significant statistics about church attendance and church decline in recent years. Here are just some UK findings:

- Nearly half (48 per cent) of our churches have fewer than five under-16-year-olds in their congregation.[34]
- There are six adults for every child or young person in a church.[35]
- Ninety per cent of adults in churches today attended as children.[36]
- Seventy-two per cent of Christian adults say that they came to faith before the age of 20. When asked how they came to faith, six per cent cite Alpha, Christianity Explored or similar courses, and 52 per cent cite growing up in a Christian home or church environment.[37]
- If people belong in church by the time they're in their 20s, they will probably stay for the rest of their lives.[38]

Such statistics can make uncomfortable reading, but there is a way to view them as prophetic. It is clear from these figures that faith will only stick where there is a context, namely where adults and children live out their faith alongside each other in a church or at home, and where children are part of the gathered church community. This is exactly the new wineskin of church that Messy Church offers us. Here, children grow up with a sense of belonging to the wider family of the church and do not have to find their way back in again, having been separated from it in a Sunday school or through a particular youth programme. These figures also make it clear that one of the key focuses for Christian faith nurture is the home itself, so equipping young adults to pass on faith at home must become a priority for the church. This focus is being worked out in practice as families are encouraged to explore faith together in expressions of church such as Messy Church.

THE ALL-AGE FACTOR

Bringing the different age groups together in order to pass on faith is, of course, the whole point of Messy togetherness. It is a holistic way of working with children and families—a factor that even our secular society recognises as offering a better way to approach social needs within the welfare system. A vital component of the Messy Church ethos is that it offers something for all ages, from cradle to old age.

Our Christian response to the needs of families in the past has been to isolate the generations from each other, trying to meet their needs without reference to the wider family context in which individuals find themselves. There are many families of children, parents and grandchildren who have become estranged because of work and educational pressures, broken relationships and long distances, as people have had to travel to find jobs.

For the healthy flourishing of human life, we all need contact with significant people of different ages; this applies to children, teenagers, young adults, those in midlife and senior citizens. The siloed approach to meeting the diverse needs of families cannot deliver everything, and Messy Church has been at the forefront of reminding us how important it is to make connections between age groups within a community. Here's a flavour of those connections from my journal, describing a Messy Church I visited in east London.

'Today's theme was love, exploring the two great commandments given to us by Jesus. There were over 40 of us there, of all ages—including teenagers and men. And it was such a relaxed and happy atmosphere that it felt to me to be one of the safest and most relationship-filled Messy Churches I have visited for a while. This church almost closed five years ago, with a congregation then of six elderly people. Today I was part of a new, refreshed congregation, 700 per cent larger. This congregation was from the estate. Some children there were "accompanied" by not-much-older teenage "siblings". For example, I chatted with one young girl who brought not only her new pet puppy (a cute Highland Terrier which was a birthday present) but also her brother, Danny. This is her family. This Messy congregation included teenagers who enjoyed the simple crafts with their extended family.

Clearly some family lives here are very chaotic. At the meal table I had a long talk with one older man whose flat had been raided four times recently by the police, who were searching for a known criminal who used to live there. It seems they just will not believe he is innocent. Today he had invited along his brother, who came with his young son. The brother only sees his son at weekends and brings him to Messy Church because he wants to do something important and special with him. For the meal, we all sat to eat around a huge "family table" in the centre of the hall.'

The sort of togetherness made possible in Messy Church is vital for messy families today. It provides a safe haven within the increasing pressures of everyday life; also, it's within this context that faith can be lived out in the real world and shared honestly with the two or three generations who have not yet heard about God's love in Christ.

THE CHURCH FACTOR

The final reason why Messy Church and similar all-age congregational models are prophetically signposting the way forward is that they are linked to a changing understanding of church itself. What would you say makes a church a church? Is it primarily a gathering of those who have been baptised as infants or adults and share in Holy Communion together? Is it simply a congregation of people who can say with conviction that they are 'born again'? Is it about loyalty to a particular liturgical format or membership of an electoral roll? Is it about depth of commitment, marked by how much money people give or their involvement in discipleship groups beyond Sunday? Is it all these things or none… or something more?

A growing understanding among many Christians is that church is made up of people on a God-inspired journey of faith together. This is the pilgrimage model, conjuring up the image of people of all ages on a walk together, some ahead and some behind; some stopping to admire the view and then hurrying to catch up; some in conversation and some walking alone but still part of the group; and some moving from one group to another to make new friends and hear new stories. Just as on any pilgrimage walk, the original group of walkers can get stretched out, so every now and again there needs to be a moment when those ahead wait for everyone to regroup, to continue the journey. It's messy, but this is what happens in real life.

This sort of understanding of church is found in Messy Church, where people are at different stages of faith and friendship with each other. Messy Church provides us with a new, contemporary understanding of how church will look increasingly in the future. It is held together by its key values, expressed during and beyond the times when people gather. Thus, Messy Church is a group of people experiencing generous hospitality around the stories of God; it is an emerging community of people trying to love and serve one another; it is a church that meets around a sacramental meal, whether that includes the elements of bread and wine or not; it is a church where faith is intentionally shared with all who come through the doors; it is a style of church that is beginning to discover what it means to learn with and from each other and where the hierarchies inherited from the past are slowly being broken down. This is the messy togetherness of intergenerational church.

CONCLUSION

Messy Church is particularly shaped by the value of togetherness, which is a vital dimension to faith nurture that we are rediscovering in the 21st century. This togetherness is expressed in a number of other ways, too.

- Firstly, it is seen in the fact that the Messy Church network goes beyond denominations, traditions and churchmanship.

- Secondly, Messy Churches are often led by ecumenical teams who are risk takers, mistake makers, ground breakers and good news bringers. These leaders are open about their weaknesses and failures; they are willing to share their successes without pride and their doubts and questions without fear.
- Thirdly, Messy togetherness is expressed in the fact that this church is both child-centred and adult-focused at the same time, giving everyone permission to be open to new things as well as drawing on received wisdom.
- Finally, Messy Church advocates are passionate not only about sharing God's love but also about receiving God's love from the wider community beyond the usual church borders. Messy Churches are safe places for Christians to meet the world, where Christians are also challenged to reframe the timeless truths of God in the language and within the context of the 21st century.

There is no doubt that Messy Church is helping to redefine outsiders' views both of church and of Christians, while at the same time giving Christians the opportunity to reimagine worship, participation, inclusion, leadership, evangelism, discipleship, children's and youth work, as well as family and all-age ministry for our day and age. Messy Church is indeed a revival in our day—but not one that seeks to separate off and set up a new movement in isolation. Rather, it allows churches to grow new life from within. It is much messier doing it that way, of course, but at least we stay together.

PART 3

MESSY TOGETHERNESS EXPLORED THROUGH THREE MESSY CHURCH SESSIONS

Every Messy Church session should be a celebration of our togetherness, as I hope I have shown throughout the chapters of this book. The crafts and activities, the gathered celebration and the meal around the table are all opportunities to bring the age groups together around the story of God's love to us in Jesus Christ. However, there are some Bible stories that especially focus on this intergenerational togetherness.

In this final section of the book, I have picked out three such stories from across the Bible. For each one, there is a fully worked-out session outline that you might like to use in your own Messy Church. In each of the three Bible stories, all ages come together—in formal, gathered celebration; at a special family occasion; and on a regular basis as a local church where everyone's gifts are welcomed and received. In each case, we find the spiritual chemistry of old and young sharing in the worship and service of God, illustrating the importance of nurturing faith through togetherness rather than in separate age groups. This is the context in which to grow a faith that can put down deep roots and endure.

SESSION 1

A SHELTER FOR ALL

An Old Testament Messy Church session

Bible story: Based on the story in Nehemiah 8:1–18
Context: A formal gathered celebration at the end of a major church building project
Theme: Building up the people of God
Key verse: 'The people were glad because God had given them great joy. The women and children were also very happy. The joyful sound in Jerusalem could be heard far away' (Nehemiah 12:43, NIRV)

HOW DOES THIS SESSION HELP PEOPLE GROW IN THEIR FAITH?

The account of how God moved Nehemiah to leave his comfortable job at the court of the Persian king, to return to his homeland and project-manage the rebuilding of Jerusalem's walls, has always been a well-loved Bible story. The book that bears Nehemiah's name is, in effect, his personal diary of how God inspired each step of the rebuilding, which, remarkably, was completed in just under two months. He was a humble man who recognised that it was by God's help that he was able to lift the spirits of those who had returned from exile, spurring them on to work together to repair the walls of their ancient capital city. They overcame opposition and discouragement from neighbouring tribal leaders, as well as internal disagreements.

In chapter 8 we find the story of the great celebration that took place as they all gathered—young and old—in front of the Water Gate to hear God's word read by the priest Ezra, to respond in repentant prayer, and to eat and drink together. They recreated shelters on the rooftops and in the courtyards as a reminder of how God had looked after them when they were wandering across the desert on their journey to the promised land.

All the elements of Messy Church are here—Bible story, prayer, food, creativity and, of course, the generations worshipping and working together. It must have been an occasion that even the very youngest would always remember, because they were part of a glorious messy togetherness that brought them all close to God again after many years of rebellion and exile. The celebration continued over many days, allowing the older members of the congregation to share a prayer that recalled all that God had done with his people from the very beginning (Nehemiah 9). Over the eight days of the festival, there were times for singing God's praises as well as expressing sadness for the way they had let God down; there were feasting and fasting; there was a time for listening to God's word being read, as well as opportunities for families to work together in response to what they heard.

Special occasions such as these, where all the generations come together, are important both for our own faith development and for discovering our place within the bigger picture of God's love and purposes for this world. No wonder the joy and singing coming from Jerusalem could be heard a long way off.

ACTIVITIES

Build a den

You will need blankets, sheets, old curtains, pegs/clips, chairs, tables, clothes rails, and anything that can be used to make a den large enough for a family group to get inside. If you have the space, there could be several dens built by the various groups at your Messy Church.

God's people built shelters to live in during the Festival of Booths while they listened to the teachings of God.

What special places are there in your life, where you feel you can come close to God?

Build the Water Gate

You will need lots of old packing cases, cardboard and strong tape. You could also use some sheets of coloured wrapping paper (perhaps in blue) to decorate the Water Gate. This is a group activity, to be worked on by families over the course of the session.

Not only had the walls of Jerusalem been broken down but also the gates had been burned and needed rebuilding. Everyone gathered in front of the Water Gate to hear God's word being read by Ezra.

How welcoming is the gate/door/entrance at your Messy Church? How might it be improved?

Gate cakes

Decorate plain fairy cakes with coloured icing. Top the icing with icing shapes that represent some of the different gates of the city: sheep gate, fountain gate, horse gate, rubbish gate, valley gate, fish gate and water gate.

The new walls created a safe place, but there also needed to be ways in and out of the city, and they needed to be guarded carefully to prevent enemies from getting in.

Why do you think the gates had these different names? What nicknames could you give the various doors and entrances at your Messy Church?

Make a brick

You will need a paddling pool, a mixture of soil, sand and clay, washing-up bowls with soapy water, towels, takeaway trays with lids and labels for lids. Invite people to take off shoes and socks and tread down the brick mixture. Then fill a tray to make an individual brick for each family to take away. Put the lid on and let the brick dry out at home.

The people who built the walls in the story were not expert brick-makers. They had to learn how to do it.

How difficult is it to learn a new skill? What would help you?

Make Jerusalem safe

Set up a corner of your Messy Church with plenty of building blocks, Lego pieces and other appropriate construction materials. On a large strong surface, mark out a perimeter for the walls, including the twelve gates. Invite family groups to build the walls along your marked outline. There were also some towers, which could be added to your walls.

It took Nehemiah and his team 52 days to complete the rebuilding of the wall. Everyone got involved, sometimes repairing the wall near to where they lived and sometimes helping out wherever else there was a need.

What different jobs might each member of the family do, depending on their age?

Ezra's book

You will need long strips of paper, plenty of narrow cardboard tubes, crayons, paste, felts, paints and ribbon. The book that Ezra read from was probably in the form of a scroll. Lay out a long strip of paper and attach a cardboard tube at each end. Roll the tubes and paper in towards the centre. You might like to paste in a preprinted song of praise from the story, such as the one recorded in Nehemiah 9:5. Decorate the scroll and tie it with ribbon to hold it together.

When Ezra and the others prayed and reminded everyone of how God had kept them throughout history, there is a recurring phrase: 'But you loved them very much'. (Nehemiah 9:19–31, NIRV). God's love never gives up.

What encouraging words would you want to read out from your scroll to your friends and family?

A wall of prayer

On a large piece of plain paper, draw outlines that suggest the shapes of bricks in a wall. Invite families to write, on rectangular sticky notes, special prayers for safety for those facing trouble and difficult circumstances.

Here is the prayer with which Nehemiah ends his Jerusalem diary: 'You are my God. Please remember me with kindness' (Nehemiah 13:31, NIRV).

Who needs to know that God will keep them safe today?

A Messy family tree

You will need chubby wax crayons, felt-tip pens, colouring pencils, pencils, paper, paints, paintbrushes, glue sticks and the shape of a large tree. Invite families to draw, paint or write their family tree on to pieces of light green card, which they will then paste on to the large Messy Church family tree.

Nehemiah is fond of making lists in his diary. There are registers of all the families who were invited back to Jerusalem and worked on the walls together. Nehemiah is not interested just in rebuilding with bricks and mortar but in bringing together the whole family of God again after years of exile. Messy Church is about creating a new community around the story of Jesus.

I wonder just how big the family of the church is. Who do you know who is part of another church, somewhere else in the world?

Family groups

You will need sets of pegs to make families of peg dolls, along with fabric for clothes, felt-tips to colour in faces, and wool for hair. In order to stand the family groups up, use some polystyrene or flower oasis. These family groups could then be placed within the walls made from construction materials, as described in the 'Make Jerusalem safe' activity.

The groups that gathered in the square before the Water Gate included all ages—anyone who could understand what was being said. It was an intergenerational occasion. Some of the priests came round to talk with the groups, to explain what they were hearing.

What has been your best experience of worshipping God together as a family?

Food to share

In your publicity for this Messy Church session, invite every family to bring along one non-perishable food item that they can give away. During Messy Church, invite families to design and write greetings cards to go with their gifts. It would be good to link this activity with your church's food bank.

In the story, families celebrated not only in the square but also back in their homes, where they shared their food with those who were in need. They realised that this is also part of our worship of God (Nehemiah 8:10, 12).

In what ways can we express our worship of God, other than by singing and praying?

CELEBRATION

Gather everyone for the celebration, using an appropriate song for the occasion. Here are some suggested words, sung to the tune of 'Bob the Builder'.

Nehemiah
Can we fix it?
Nehemiah
Yes, we can

Nehemiah
Can we build it?
Nehemiah
Yes, we can

Nehemiah
Can God help us?
Nehemiah
Yes, God can

Nehemiah
Can we thank him?
Nehemiah
Yes, we can

As people sing and gather, build a secure high platform in the middle of your celebration area—for example, a chair on a table on a piece of staging. This is Ezra's pulpit before the Water Gate, from which he read from God's word to all the families gathered there.

Welcome everyone and draw on the various activities to help set the scene for the story.

Story outline

Open up a large version of one of the scrolls, like the ones made in the activity 'Ezra's book', and read the words below. Every time the storyteller says, 'Praise our great Lord God', everyone should shout out, 'Amen, Amen'.

God made the heavens and the earth: praise our great Lord God!
Amen, Amen

God chose Abraham and brought us into the promised land: praise our great Lord God!
Amen, Amen

God rescued us when we were slaves in Egypt: praise our great Lord God!
Amen, Amen

God showed us the way to go in the desert: praise our great Lord God!
Amen, Amen

God gave us the ten commandments: praise our great Lord God!
Amen, Amen

God looked after us by day and by night: praise our great Lord God!
Amen, Amen

Say, 'But so often we forgot to remember God. We decided we knew best. We turned away from God's love.' *(Ask everyone to pull a sad face and look down to the ground with shame.)*

'But listen to what Nehemiah told everyone: this is a special day for the Lord your God. So don't be sad and don't cry, because God loves you so much. The joy of the Lord is your strength, so praise our great Lord God!'

(Everyone says) **Amen, Amen**

'Now go back to your homes; enjoy good food and drink and share with those who don't have anything.'

Encourage all the families to gather in the shelters that they have built. Then invite one member of each family to come forward with the food item they have brought to add to the local food bank. (Have spare items ready, of course.)

Now invite everyone to gather in a circle and become the living walls of your Messy Church Jerusalem. This is a safe place for families to gather.

End the story with these words from Psalm 48:12–14. You may be able to put them up on a screen for everyone to say together. (Explain that 'Zion' is another name for Jerusalem.)

Let's walk around Zion and count its towers. We will see its strong walls and visit each fortress. Then you can say to future generations, 'Our God is like this for ever and will always guide us.'

Song

Here's a song suggestion, sung to the tune of 'The wise man built his house upon the rock'.

God's friend Nehemiah built a wall tall and strong (x3)
So the city would be safe.

The people helped to build each gate and tower (x3)
So the wall would be complete.

They prayed to the Lord to help them with the work (x3)
And he gave them joy and strength.

They listened and they prayed, as they gathered one and all (x3)
'and praised their great Lord God!'

Prayers

As everyone stands in a large family circle, use the following prayer suggestions:

Help us, Lord, to care for each other in this Messy community. (Invite everyone to reach out to each side, placing hands across each other's shoulders.)

Help us, Lord, to be strong for the week ahead. (Invite everyone to link up elbows.)

Help us, Lord, to welcome each other and be good friends to our neighbours. (Invite everyone to hold hands.)

Help us, Lord, to trust in you, each and every day. (Invite everyone to continue holding hands but lift them high.)

Praise our great Lord God! Amen, Amen

End with the Messy Grace (with actions).

MEAL SUGGESTION

- Fish fingers, chips, bread and butter
- Gate cakes (made in the activity session)

TAKE-HOME IDEA

Place your 'takeaway' brick somewhere in your home to remind you of Nehemiah and today's story. When you listen to or watch the news and hear about cities that are caught up in war, hold the brick and say a prayer to God to help the families there.

SESSION 2

A FAMILY FOR ALL

A Messy Church session from the Gospels

Bible story: Based on the story in Luke 2:22–38

Context: A special family occasion such as a baptism or dedication

Theme: Jesus draws together the different generations in the community

Key verse: 'Anna came in and praised God. She spoke about the child Jesus to everyone' (Luke 2:38).

HOW DOES THIS SESSION HELP PEOPLE GROW IN THEIR FAITH?

This story in Luke 2 is quite simply about a family who wanted to say ' thank you' to God for the birth of their new baby. Mary and Joseph travel to the big city of Jerusalem and to the big 'church' there called the temple. At this dedication service, an elderly man and an elderly woman have some surprising things to say and do, which the baby's parents will never forget.

The relationship between those of grandparent age and the children in a church can be a very important one, and the special bond that often exists across the generations can play a vital role in helping children to grow up into a mature faith. Although Simeon and Anna in this story were not related to Jesus by blood, they can be seen as his spiritual grandparents. They rejoice at his birth, for which they have long hoped; they foresee the special purposes of his life and they can't help but tell others of the news of his arrival. Proud grandparents indeed!

This story is celebrated in many Christian traditions at the feast of Candlemas, which comes at the beginning of February, six weeks after Christmas. I have always been drawn to icons of this Bible story, known as 'The Presentation'. In the picture there is 'great-grandma' Anna and 'grandad' Simeon, along with the older stepdad Joseph and the teenage mother Mary. In the middle is the child Jesus, bringing the generations together. It is a family picture, although only two of them are related by blood. It's a messy family but it is made holy by the presence of Jesus.

This messy togetherness is also a vehicle for mission to the world, as expressed in Simeon's song, which proclaims Jesus as the 'light to lighten the Gentiles', and in the response of Anna, who sets out to tell everyone in Jerusalem about Jesus. It is also interesting to note that the event involving this messy missionary family took place in a corner of the temple and probably went unnoticed by the majority of the worshippers that day, just as, so often, Messy Church continues its special intergenerational mission on the margins of inherited church.

ACTIVITIES

Messy family photos

Set up a photo booth in one corner of your Messy Church and invite two families at a time to come together for a group picture. (You will need to get permission for this, of course, from those participating.) Mix everyone up so that the friendship and blood connections between the people involved are blurred. Ask one person from the group to hold a baby doll in his or her hands. If it is possible, you could show the resulting pictures on a screen at the beginning of your celebration. You may also be able to print them off or email them to the families involved.

In today's story the baby Jesus brings together people from different family groups across the generations to create a new messy family.

How big would your family friendship tree be?

Build part of the temple

You will need lots of old packing cases, cardboard and strong tape. You could also use some sheets of coloured wrapping paper to decorate the section of the temple that you create. Perhaps you could focus on the great steps up to the entrance, with the two tall pillars either side. This is a group activity to be worked on by families over the course of the session.

It must have been an overpowering experience for Mary and Joseph to carry baby Jesus up into the grandeur of the temple, compared with the humble home they had made for themselves in Bethlehem.

How might you feel, arriving at the temple in Jerusalem, knowing that your baby was someone special from God?

Make a Moses basket

You will need paper, scissors, glue and strong construction

paper. You can find instructions for a woven paper 'Moses basket' at www.dltk-bible.com/crafts/mbasketweave.htm.

Jesus probably arrived at the temple in a baby carrier, such as a Moses basket. Like Moses, he had come to rescue God's people and, as God's Son, he was being brought up by a 'borrowed' human family. According to Old Testament law, the firstborn child belonged to God. This was especially true of Jesus.

Have you ever been to a baptism or dedication for a baby? What happened?

A pair of pigeons

You will need air-drying clay, salt dough or playdough. Mould the clay or dough into the shape of two small pigeons. Have some pictures of pigeons from the internet to give people an idea of what to do. Draw on lines to represent the wings and feathers, and use small beads for the eyes. Leave the models to dry. Salt dough can be hardened quickly in a microwave, enabling families to paint their finished birds.

For the dedication service in the temple, families were expected to bring a gift to sacrifice. Mary and Joseph could only bring the cheapest gift of two young pigeons.

What gifts do we bring to church when we come to worship?

Babies in blankets

You will need some packets of Nice biscuits, icing, food colouring and a packet of jelly babies. Roll out different-coloured icing and cut out blanket shapes to place on the Nice biscuit. Create some pillows, too, and then tuck in a jelly baby to 'sleep' soundly.

The baby Jesus was only six weeks old when he arrived at the temple for this special service.

I wonder if the baby Jesus cried when Simeon sang and Anna got so excited.

Simeon's song

From various Bible translations, prayer books and the internet, collect as many different versions of Simeon's song as you can find. (Many of these will be musical arrangements or rhyming poetry.) Lay them out on a table and invite families to choose which versions they like best. On a chalkboard, they can create a new version of the song, inspired by the ideas in front of them. Also have some paper available for people to make their own picture of Simeon singing about the baby.

In some church traditions, Simeon's song is sung as part of evening worship (sometimes called the Nunc Dimittis). Simeon had waited all his life to sing it.

How do you think Simeon knew that this baby was different from all the others who had been brought to the temple, that day and over his lifetime?

A special picture

Find an icon of 'The Presentation' from the internet and print it off, as large as you can. Mount it on card with a large border, where people can stick prayer notes, and rest the card on an easel. Use it as the focus for a prayer station.

Write out some simple wondering questions, such as: Which part of this icon do you like the best? Where is the light coming from in this icon? What do you find strange about this icon? Can you identify who everyone is? Where would you stand if you were part of this picture? What does this icon tell you about God? How does this icon make you feel?

A sword cross

You will need a sword template, strong card, silver foil, scissors, sticky tape, paste, felt-tip pens and some shiny sequins. Draw around the template on card and cut out the sword. Wrap silver foil around the blade. Colour the handle and decorate it with sequins on one side. On the other side, colour and decorate the handle and just part of the blade, to make a cross shape.

After Simeon had sung his song, he spoke words of prophecy about Jesus. Jesus would divide people's allegiance, and Mary's joy over her baby's birth would become an experience of sadness and pain. It seems that Simeon was pointing forward to what would happen on Good Friday, when Mary watched her son die on the cross.

Do you think Mary understood what Simeon meant by his strange words?

Just a minute

Play a challenge game. This story is about people who dedicated their lives to looking out for God's moment. Imagine waiting up to 84 years for your time to go out and do 'street evangelism'!

Play some waiting games with families—for example, one in which individuals guess whether a certain amount of time has elapsed. Invite groups to sit down, and then ask them to stand up when they think a certain number of seconds have passed. Begin with short periods like 15, 20 or

40 seconds, and work up towards one minute or two. Who is the closest to being correct each time?

Light for the world

You will need some cheap packs of glowsticks from a pound shop. You will also need some plastic globes. Using marker pens, colour the globes in blue and green so that they give the impression of being small model worlds. Snap the glow-sticks and wrap them around the globes. Use tape to secure the sticks in place.

When Jesus grew up, perhaps Mary told him about Simeon's song and prophecy. Jesus called himself 'the light of the world', which picks up Simeon's description of him as 'the light that lightens the Gentiles'.

In what ways does Jesus light up the world, do you think?

CELEBRATION

Gather everyone for the celebration using some appropriate music, such as 'This little light of mine' (*Junior Praise*) or 'Walk in the light' (the chorus from 'The Spirit lives to set us free', *Kidsource*).

Welcome everyone and draw on the various activities to help set the scene for the story.

In order to tell the Bible story for this session, use two visual aids from the activity tables—a Moses basket and the steps and doors or other part of the temple. Dress up one grandad to be Simeon and one granny to be Anna, using two appropriately coloured dressing-gowns.

Story outline

Mary and Joseph were so excited. They had been given the gift of a baby boy. Jesus was their miracle child, promised by God and named by the angels. After six weeks, it was time to take the baby to Jerusalem, the capital of their country, to visit the temple for a special thanksgiving service. They wanted to offer their baby back to God, and they brought a special gift to dedicate him to God's service.

Mary and Joseph arrived in the busy city and made their way through its streets to the huge and impressive temple building. There were many steps to climb in order to reach the courts where they would have the special service for their child. It must have been overwhelming for them, compared with the small village they had come from.

As the service started, an elderly man arrived. When he saw the baby, his eyes lit up. With permission from Mary, he took the baby into his arms and began to sing a song. He sang that this was God's special rescuer, come to bring hope to Israel and the whole world. The baby would be a light that would lighten up everyone's lives. He warned Mary that her heart would one day be broken by what happened to her child, but also said that many people would be rescued by him.

Here's a simple short version of Simeon's song. Perhaps you could make up a tune to go with it.

Now I can go in peace
and my long waiting cease.
God's rescuer has come,
a light for everyone.

Just after Simeon had finished singing, a great-granny called Anna arrived. She too had been on the look-out for God's special rescuer, and she became very excited when she heard Simeon's song and saw the baby Jesus. She began to rush around and tell everyone she met that God had kept his promise, and that Jesus was the child they'd all been waiting for.

What a surprise that day was for Mary and Joseph! What a surprise it was for the people of Jerusalem! God had taken the world by surprise by sending Jesus. God's rescue came in a most unexpected way and through the most unexpected people. This messy family group in the temple was the start of a massive change for the whole world.

Song

Picking up on the theme of Jesus as the light of the world and the enthusiasm of Anna, choose from the following:

- Verse 1 and the chorus of 'Lord, the light of your love is shining' (*Mission Praise*)
- Verses 1 and 2 of 'Go tell it on the mountain' (*Mission Praise*)
- 'This little light of mine' (*Junior Praise*)

Prayers

Make sure everyone can see a circular piece of white felt, on which you place two tall pillar candles and a small tealight. Light the candles carefully and say that they are going to represent the grandad and great-granny from our story—Simeon and Anna—and the baby Jesus.

Jesus is the light. He is the hope that lit up Anna and Simeon's lives and he is the hope for the whole world.

The candles can also represent all the grandparents and children in our Messy Church. In a moment of quiet, encourage the children and teenagers to pray for all the parents and grandparents, and the grandparents and parents for all the children and teenagers. Whether the candles are tall or small, the same light of Jesus can burn as bright for both.

Thank you, Jesus, that you came to be the light for grandparents and grandchildren, for young and old, for me and for those I love. Amen

End with the Messy Grace (with actions).

MEAL SUGGESTION

- Lasagne and peas
- Jelly and ice cream

TAKE-HOME IDEA

Draw up a simple Messy Church family tree at home, with the names not only of those from your own family but also of the other parents, grandparents and great-grandparents who are part of your Messy Church.

Grandparents often have inherited skills and crafts that they can pass on to their grandchildren. Find out what the grandparents and great-grandparents in your Messy Church know about, and arrange an opportunity for those skills and memories to be passed on. Perhaps this could be an activity table at your next Messy Church.

In a similar way, children know many things that they can teach their grandparents and great-grandparents, particularly in the field of technology. Arrange an opportunity for the children to teach the older generation how to do something on a computer or camera phone.

Talk about what Jesus the child meant to Anna and Simeon, and what Mary the mother learnt from these surprise spiritual grandparents.

SESSION 3

A HOME FOR ALL

A Messy Church session from the epistles

Bible story: Based on 1 Corinthians 12:12–27
Context: Any regular gathering of the local church
Theme: Everyone, young and old, has a role to play in the ministry and mission of the church
Key verse: 'Together you are the body of Christ. Each one of you is part of his body' (1 Corinthians 12:27)

HOW DOES THIS SESSION HELP PEOPLE GROW IN THEIR FAITH?

The apostle Paul uses the image of a human body more than once in his letters to help his readers understand how the church should work. Our bodies are made up of many different parts, each with their own particular functions and vital contribution to the overall health of a person. Some of these parts are very visible and, superficially at least, seem to be more significant, but in fact our hidden organs and blood vessels beneath the skin are just as important, if not more so. Paul transfers these ideas to illustrate how every single person is important and has a part to play in making Christ known.

We sometimes forget, however, that Paul's letters to the

churches in places like Rome, Philippi and Corinth were read out to the whole gathered congregation. These weren't private, specialist communications to particular leaders or age groups in those churches. Everyone heard what Paul had to say, and they understood that his words were for everyone—including household slaves, women, children and even some of 'the outsiders' who were perhaps 'just looking' when it came to the matter of faith in Jesus.

When we hear what Paul has to say about the church being the body of Christ, any of those listening might well be the hand, foot, eyes or ears that he is talking about. There is no sense here that only those who have reached a certain level of spiritual maturity are qualified to be particular limbs. In fact, the whole thrust of what Paul is saying is that some of the least likely members of a congregation may well be the most significant parts of Christ's body, the church.

Messy Church fully embraces this idea of 'every-member ministry' with its emphasis on the importance of team leadership and the valuing of young and old in the togetherness that makes this fresh expression of church possible.

ACTIVITIES

Newspaper people

You will need lots of newspapers and some sticky tape. Work in groups to create a person out of the newspapers, rolling together sheets and attaching the head, body and limbs with tape. Some family groups might like to add a hat to the finished model.

In three of his letters Paul uses the image of a body to help us understand what the church is like (see Romans 12:1–8; 1 Corinthians 12:2–27; Ephesians 4:1–13).

What are the advantages of understanding church as a body rather than a building?

Design a church

You will need lots of polystyrene packaging pieces and blunted cocktail sticks. Design a church using the pieces and sticks—not a building necessarily, but what a church could be. How big can you make it? Is everyone at the table making separate models or one all together? Are they better apart or together? What holds the church together? What breaks it up?

What is the most important aspect of a church, as far as you're concerned?

Rainbow people

You will need to buy some ready-made gingerbread people or ask someone at Messy Church to make some. You will also need icing and food colouring. Decorate each section of a gingerbread person in a different colour.

'God's rainbow people' could well be a description for the church, with each person contributing his or her own special colour to the overall body of Christ.

In what ways is this Messy Church a rainbow of different people?

A beautiful flower

You will need thin strips of coloured paper, pencils, card and paste (or purchase some quilling sets). Twirl a flower from the paper strips (making it curl using the body of the pencil) and stick it on to card to represent the growth and beauty that God wants to bring to his church and his world.

It's exciting when we see families growing in the love of God and when we see churches blossoming like a flower with new life.

How is this Messy Church blossoming for God?

Skeleton bodies

You will need packets of broad craft sticks, a sharp implement to make holes and split-pin fasteners. Prepare the craft sticks beforehand by making a hole at each end. Invite families to design their own skeleton bodies with the craft sticks and pin all the parts together so they become jointed and movable.

Teresa of Avila famously said that 'Christ has no body now but ours, no hands and feet but ours'. Each one of us is part of Christ's body and each of us can be the hands and feet of Jesus for others.

Which part of a church, do you think, is like the hands of Jesus? Which part is like the feet?

Body art

You will need paper, pencils, crayons and felt-tips. Invite families to doodle different parts of a human body. Which part of the body of this church do you feel you are or could be? Draw it and write on the shape why you think it represents you. Can you link your drawing to the parts of the body drawn by others?

The apostle Paul said, 'Our bodies don't have just one part. They have many parts' (1 Corinthians 12:12).

Do you think some people can be more than one part of the body of the church?

Everybody prayers

Cut out some people shapes from card and draw a large outline of a human body on a piece of lining paper. Invite people to write their prayers on the people shapes and stick the shapes on the part of the large outline body that they feel is linked to their prayer for others in the church and community.

Pomander face

You will need some apples or oranges, and cloves. With the cloves, make a face on your apple or orange. Thread a piece of ribbon through a large needle and push it through the core of the fruit. Detach the needle, tie a knot in one end of the ribbon and use the other end to hang up the finished pomander.

In your church, who would you say are the eyes, the ears, the mouth, the nose, and so on? Who is the head?

The everybody challenge

You will need cardboard and plastic balls or bean bags. Cut out a large body shape from a big piece of cardboard, and mount it so that it can stand upright. Cut holes in the cardboard at the mouth, hands, knees, heart and waist.

Challenge families to see how many bean bags or balls they can get through the holes in the body within a certain time limit and from an agreed distance.

Which parts of the body of Christ do you think might be missing at this Messy Church?

The church is people

You will need plenty of glossy magazines and a large outline of the venue for your Messy Church. Invite family groups to cut out faces from the magazines and stick them on to the outline of the building, so that it is completely full by the end of the session. Try to include all sorts of faces from every age and ethnic group.

How can the church still be the church when we aren't gathered together?

CELEBRATION

Gather everyone for the celebration, using some appropriate music for this occasion, such as Fischy Music's 'Everybody's body' song (see www.fischy.com/songs/everybodys-body).

Welcome everyone and use the various activities to help set the scene for the story.

Song

Introduce the Bible story today with a song. It involves heads, shoulders, knees, toes, ears, eyes, nose and mouth.

Heads, shoulders, knees and toes, knees and toes
Heads, shoulders, knees and toes, knees and toes
Eyes and ears and mouth and nose,
Heads, shoulders, knees and toes, knees and toes

Touch each part of the body as you prepare, then sing. You can develop this nursery song further by leaving out some words each time and just touching the part of the body instead, until finally it is an almost silent song, just with the word 'and' every now and then.

Story outline

Say, 'That was a "body song"—and the church is like a body. It's made up of many people who are the body's many parts. In the Bible, the writer Paul describes a church as a human body with different parts—and every part is important. Listen to this story that Paul told about the church being the body of Christ.'

Divide your Messy congregation into two. Invite everyone to stand and wiggle different parts of the body—hands, head, feet, toes, and so on.

The body of Christ has many parts, just like our human bodies. It's not just one part that's all the same, but it is made up of many parts that are all different.

Ask one half of the congregation to wave a foot, and the other half to wave a hand.

A foot can't say, 'I'm not a hand, so I don't belong to the body.' And a hand can't say, 'I'm not a foot, so I don't belong to the body.'

Ask one half to hold on to both ears, and the other half to point to both eyes and blink a lot.

The ears can't say, 'I'm not an eye, so I don't belong to the body.' The eyes can't say, 'I'm not an ear, so I don't belong to the body.'

If our bodies were only eyes, then we couldn't hear or eat or run or play games. If our bodies were only ears, then we couldn't smell or see or taste or dance.

God has put all the parts of the body together, writes Paul, in the best possible way, so each part has a role to play.

It is the same with the church, which is Christ's body on earth. Everyone in it has a part to play.

Ask everyone to 'hide' their hands up their sleeves or behind their backs.

Our eyes can't do without our hands. How would we pick up what they see?

Ask everyone to kneel on the ground to hide their feet.

Our hands can't do without our feet. How would they reach what they want to pick up?

Ask everyone to look embarrassed and coy.

Some of the less beautiful parts of the body are the most important, and some of the less beautiful parts are vital. Just imagine not having a bottom!

Invite everyone to stand up and wave everything.

God has put together the body, wrote Paul, so that every part needs every other part. All the parts are valuable and important.

Invite everyone to hold their head as if they've got a headache.

If one part of the body hurts, it affects the whole body.

Invite everyone to do some star jumps.

What's good for one part of the body is good for the whole body. It's the same with us, writes Paul, in the church. Each one can be part of Christ's body and each one has a vital part to play.

I wonder which part of the body you are or could be.

I wonder what you're good at. Is it listening or speaking? Is it seeing what needs to be done or helping others or visiting? Is it doing something that no one else notices?

Clear a space in the middle of your congregation, or invite everyone to move to a nearby open area.

Let's draw a huge body on the ground. Then let's all come and stand on the part of that imagined body where we think we might be in the body of the church.

Prayers

Return to the theme of the song sung at the beginning, and invite everyone to touch each of the following body parts as you pray.

Head: *Thank you, Father, for people with gifts of planning and organising.*

Shoulders: *Thank you, Father, for people with gifts of taking responsibility and bearing other people's burdens.*

Knees: *Thank you, Father, for people with the gifts of praying and getting down on their knees to play with children.*

Toes: *Thank you, Father, for people with the gifts of getting things started, being pioneers, pushing the church off on a journey of mission and helping it keep a balance between mission and ministry.*

Eyes: *Thank you, Father, for people with the gifts of seeing what needs to be done and spotting those who are new and feeling lost.*

Ears: *Thank you, Father, for people with the gifts of listening to what people are really saying, and hearing what is not said.*

Mouth: *Thank you, Father, for people with the gifts of telling stories and knowing the right things to say to make visitors feel welcomed and loved.*

Nose: *Thank you, Father, for people with the gifts of creating tasty and appetising food that smells mouth-wateringly good.*

Thank you, Lord God, for giving each of us gifts to bless others in our teams, in our churches, in our communities and in our world. We are the body of Christ and individually members of it; we are all needed to be his hands and feet in this world. Amen

End with the Messy Grace (with actions).

MEAL SUGGESTION

- Sausages and mash
- Gingerbread people made during the activities, or cakes

TAKE-HOME IDEA

Before the next Messy Church, challenge each other in your family to find ways of using their hands, feet, eyes, ears and mouths to be the body of Christ at home, at school, at work or in the neighbourhood.

Each day, focus on one of these parts of the body and work out something good that you could do, which would please God and be a blessing to others. For example, hands could carry something for a person who is struggling; feet could go on an errand for someone who is housebound; eyes could help someone who is blind to cross the road, and so on.

APPENDIX 1

FURTHER READING ON INTERGENERATIONAL CHURCH, WORSHIP AND LEARNING

Over the past 40 years, a number of seminal books have explored the nature of all-age worship, usually in the context of how it can be worked out as one particular form of service on a Sunday morning, perhaps once a month. Messy Church differs from this model in that the default setting is always all-age rather than having separate age groups for worship and learning, and it does not start by trying to fit all-age into existing traditional liturgical service patterns.

The present-day movement towards all-age worship, ministry and mission is one that can be identified in a number of documents and publications over the last decade, including the following:

I. Beckwith, *Postmodern Children's Ministry* (Zondervan, 2004).

Philip Mounstephen and Kelly Martin, *Body Beautiful? Recapturing a vision for all-age church* (Grove, 2004).

P. Meyers, *Live, Learn, Pass It On: The practical benefits of generations growing together in faith* (Discipleship Resources, 2006).

J. Roberto, 'Best practices in intergenerational faith formation', *Lifelong Faith*, 1(3) (2007), pp. 5–16

C. Ross, 'Being an intergenerational congregation', *Issues*, 41(2) (2007), pp. 24–32.

Mariette Martineau, Joan Webe and Leif Kehrwald, *Intergenerational Faith Formation: All ages learning together* (Twenty-Third Publications, 2008)

Holly Catterton Allen and Christine Lawton Ross, *Intergenerational Christian Formation: Bringing the whole church together in ministry, community and worship* (IVP, 2012)

Vern Bengtson, *Families and Faith: How religion is passed down across generations* (Oxford University Press, 2013)

Kathie Amidei, Jim Merhaut and John Roberto, *Generations Together: Caring, praying, learning, celebrating and serving faithfully* (Lifelong Faith Associates, 2014)

John Roberto, *Reimagining Faith Formation for the 21st Century* (Lifelong Faith Associates, 2015)

The Family Ministry Research Project (CGMC and the Methodist Church, 2014–15): www.cgmcontheweb.com

Unfinished Business (CGMC, a network of Churches Together in Britain and Ireland), available at www.cgmcontheweb.com

Keith J. White, *The Growth of Love* (BRF, 2008) and *The Study Guide to The Growth of Love*, available from Mill Grove: www.millgrove.org.uk/publications

Other recent books that offer guidelines and service outlines for all-age acts of worship include the following:

Nick Harding, *Top Tips on All-Age Worship* (SU, 2005)

Nick Harding, *All-Age Everything: Worship for an intergenerational church* (Kevin Mayhew, 2009)

Sandra Millar, *Worship Together: Creating all-age services that work* (SPCK, 2012)

Sandra Millar, *Festivals Together: Creating all-age worship through the year* (SPCK, 2012)

Karen Morrison, *Creative Ideas for All-Age Church* (Barnabas, 2010)

Related websites include the following:

- www.barnabasinchurches.org.uk
- www.churchofengland.org/education/adult-education-lay-discipleship-and-shared-ministry/learning-for-all-ages.aspx
- www.faithformationlearningexchange.net
- www.lifelongfaith.com
- www.messychurch.org.uk
- www.reimaginefaithformation.com
- www.rootsontheweb.com
- www.scriptureunion.org.uk/shop/churchandministryresources/allageworship/10043.id

APPENDIX 2

RESOURCES FOR INTERGENERATIONAL CHURCH

- Messy Church and all the related resources and books: www.brfonline.org.uk
- Baker Ross starter packs: www.messychurch.org.uk/resource/baker-ross-messy-church-craft-boxes
- CPO Messy Church resources: www.messychurch.org.uk/resource/cpo-publicity-resources-merchandise
- 'Authorised Mess': Books of the Bible Messy sessions written by 66 Messy Churches celebrating the 400th anniversary of the King James Bible: www.messychurch.org.uk/resource/authorised-mess
- *Get Messy!* magazine: www.messychurch.org.uk/resources/get-messy
- Messy Church Facebook page: www.facebook.com/messychurchBRF
- Messy Church Pinterest page: www.pinterest.com/MessyChurchBRF
- Free monthly Messy Church e-news (subscription): www.messychurch.org.uk/newsletter
- An example of a Messy Church family registration form for Messy Church sessions: www.messychurch.org.uk/resource/registration-form

- Messy Church planning grid: www.messychurch.org.uk/resource/messy-church-planning-grid
- Best ways to email and text: www.messychurch.org.uk/resource/how-messy-churches-can-make-best-use-email-and-small-print
- Lots of ideas, especially to help with Messy celebrations: www.barnabasinchurches.org.uk/ideas
- Christian faith with families at home (good for takeaway sheets): www.faithinhomes.org.uk
- Who Let The Dads Out? BRF's ministry supporting dads and preschool children: www.wholetthedadsout.org.uk
- Great wooden crafts, Big Beautiful Tree and more Messy seasonal resources: www.inf.co.uk
- Local stores for art materials and business cast-offs: www.scrapstoresuk.org
- Popular with Sunday schools and Messy Churches: www.activityvillage.co.uk
- Ideas for science and for older children: http://ngkids.co.uk/science-and-nature and http://pbskids.org/zoom/activities/sci
- Activities and challenges (alternative to crafts): www.nbc.com/minute-to-win-it
- Table Talk, including Table Talk for Messy moments: www.table-talk.org
- Talks, PowerPoints, activity sheets and so on: www.sermons4kids.com, www.whatsinthebible.com and http://flamecreativekids.blogspot.co.uk

- PowerPoints: www.pppst.com and www.freebibleimages.org
- Variety of resources including edible Christmas: www.childrensministry.org.au
- Puppet scripts by various authors: www.puppetresources.com
- Downloadable Bible stories in various formats, including PowerPoint: www.bibleforchildren.org

Art and craft supplies

- www.bakerross.co.uk
- www.hobbycraft.co.uk
- www.craftycrocodiles.co.uk
- www.ss-services.co.uk
- www.littlecraftybugs.co.uk
- www.crafts4christians.co.uk
- www.wooden-crosses.co.uk

Songs

- www.fischy.com
- www.outoftheark.co.uk

Books and videos

- www.lostsheep.com.au

Craft ideas

- www.daniellesplace.com
- www.crayola.com
- www.dltk-bible.com

Programme material

- www.rootsontheweb.com/Find_out_more/ROOTS_Adult_and_All_Age_resources
- www.seasonsonline.ca
- www.scriptureunion.org.uk/43752.id

APPENDIX 3

HEALTH CHECK FOR A MESSY CHURCH

Welcome

- Is your Messy Church well signposted? Is it easy for visitors to find where to go? Is there a welcome information sheet or equivalent?
- Do you offer a good welcome at the door?
- Is everyone welcomed and the theme for the day explained?
- Is everyone welcomed at the activity tables and encouraged to participate?
- Is everyone welcomed in the celebration and helped to feel part of it all?
- Is everyone welcomed at the meal and offered friendship?

Activities

- Are the activities well signposted?
- Do you encourage all ages to join in?
- Are the activities for adults as well as children?

- Is there a range of activities for different types of learners/ages/interests?
- Are the activities creative and exciting, suited to differing learning and spiritual styles?
- Are any types of activity missing?
- Do the activities help people to explore the theme?
- Is the theme clear?
- Do you encourage people to talk about the activities and the theme?
- Is God-talk encouraged?

Celebration

- Is it clear where to go and what is happening?
- Are the songs appropriate and relevant to people with some faith or no faith?
- Is the Bible story told?
- Is it for all ages?
- Is the celebration Christ-centred?
- Are there opportunities to get involved?
- Is there an opportunity for reflection and prayer?
- How does the celebration connect with the activities and the theme?

Meal

- Is the meal for everyone?
- How easy is it to find out where to go, what to do and where to sit?
- What are the conversations at the table like?
- Are friendships being made?
- Are there opportunities for God-talk?
- Do people sit together in family groups or do they mix?
- How easy is it to get to meet new people?
- What are the serving arrangements?
- What sort of community-building is going on (for example, birthdays, announcements, celebrations, invitations to other events, take-home sheets and so on)?

General

- What is your team's overall evaluation of your Messy Church experience?
- Was a sense of community being built?
- How is your Messy Church congregation made up (church people, team, new people, children, teenagers, adults, visitors from other churches and so on)?
- How well is the Christian story being shared?
- Can people grow in their faith here?

- Is it really all-age?
- Where is God in it all?
- What makes you go 'Wow'?
- What makes you wince?
- What makes you wonder?
- What makes you worry?
- How was this church?

NOTES

1 www.brfonline.org.uk/pdfs/messymonth_2014.pdf

2 John Westerhoff III, Households of Faith conference, Brighton, UK (July 2014)

3 Philip Mounstephen and Kelly Martin, *Body Beautiful: Recapturing a vision for all-age church* (Grove, 2004)

4 David M. Csinos and Ivy Beckwith, 'Better together: the formative power of intergenerational community', *The Journal of Family and Community Ministries*, Vol. 28, 2015

5 Beth Barnett, 'All-Age Worship: why including little ones is good for big ones too', *Children's Work* (Premier, December 2014/January 2015)

6 www.stickyfaith.org

7 For the full report and a summary paper, go to www.cgmcontheweb.com/?page_id=543 and www.methodist.org.uk/mission/families/resources/family-ministries-research-project

8 Holly Catterton Allen and Christine Lawton Ross, *Intergenerational Christian Formation* (IVP Academic, 2012)

9 James Frazier, *Across the Generations: Incorporating all ages in ministry* (Augsburg, 2001)

10 Margaret Sawin, *Family Enrichment with Family Clusters* (Judson, 1979)

11 Jane Rogers Vann, *The Church of All Ages: Generations worshipping together* (Alban Institute, 2008)

12 Kathie Amidei, Jim Merhaut and John Roberto, *Generations Together* (LifelongFaith Associates, 2014), p. 18

13 Holly Catterton Allen, 'Families, worship, and children's spirituality', in *Wineskins* (Summer 2004)

14 Pastor Greg, 'On choosing and using curriculum', https://formingfaith.wordpress.com/2015/04/30/on-choosing-and-using-curriculum

15 Pastor Greg, 'They told their stories', https://formingfaith.wordpress.com/2015/05/16/they-told-their-stories

16 David M. Csinos and Ivy Beckwith, *Children's Ministry in the Way of Jesus* (IVP USA, 2013)

17 Barnett, 'All-Age Worship' in *Children's Work* (December 2014/January 2015)

18 Brenda Snailum, 'Implementing intergenerational ministry within existing evangelical church congregations', *Christian Educational Journal* (Series 3), Vol. 9 No. 1 (Spring 2012)
19 David Kinnaman, *You Lost Me: Why young Christians are leaving the church... and rethinking faith* (Baker Books, 2011)
20 Lucy Moore, *All-Age Worship* (BRF, 2010), p. 36
21 Consultative Group on Ministry among Children, *Unfinished Business* paragraph 5.36 (CCBI Publications), p. 62 (available at www.cgmcontheweb.com/?page_id=41)
22 Keith J. White, *The Growth of Love* (BRF, 2008), pp. 127–129
23 Nick Harding, *All-Age Everything* (Kevin Mayhew, 2001), p. 11
24 Pete Leveson, *Faith and Society Files: 'New-Humanity' Church*, a dissertation submitted to Cliff College, p. 44: www.baptist.org.uk/Articles/366550/Faith_and_Society.aspx
25 From Joanna Collicutt and Martyn Payne, 'The ageless kingdom of God', *Church Times* (11 December 2015)
26 www.faithformationlearningexchange.net/uploads/5/2/4/6/5246709/saturation_spirituality-creating_environmentsthatnurtureallchildren_-_csinos.pdf
27 G.K. Chesterton, 'Oxford from without' in *All Things Considered* (Methuen, 1908)
28 Friedrich Fröbel, *The Education of Man* (Ulan Press, 2012)
29 See, for example, Lucy Moore, *Messy Church* (Barnabas for Children, 2006), p. 77
30 Jane Leadbetter, *Messy Prayer* (Messy Church, 2015)
31 *From Anecdote to Evidence* (Church Army, 2014)
32 Paul Moore, *Making Disciples in Messy Church* (Messy Church, 2013), pp. 19–34
33 Moore, *Making Disciples in Messy Church*, p. 47
34 Based on a survey of 11,700 Anglican churches in 2011, published 2012 by the Archbishops' Council
35 From the 'Everyone counts' survey of 600 Anglican churches in 2014, published 2015 by the Archbishops' Council
36 From *Discipleship, children and the non-churched: our Last Chance Saloon?*, research into Fresh Expressions by Revd John Walker, 2011
37 From *21st Century Evangelicals* research series by the Evangelical Alliance (2012)
38 From *From Anecdote to Evidence*

Enjoyed this book?

Write a review—we'd love to hear what you think.
Email: reviews@brf.org.uk

Keep up to date—receive details of our new books as they happen.
Sign up for email news and select your interest groups at:
www.brfonline.org.uk/findoutmore/

Follow us on Twitter @brfonline

By post—to receive new title information by post (UK only), complete the form below and post to: BRF Mailing Lists, 15 The Chambers, Vineyard, Abingdon, Oxfordshire, OX14 3FE

Your Details

Name ____________________

Address ____________________

____

Town/City __________ Post Code __________

Email ____________________

Your Interest Groups (*Please tick as appropriate)

- ☐ Advent/Lent
- ☐ Bible Reading & Study
- ☐ Children's Books
- ☐ Discipleship
- ☐ Leadership
- ☐ Messy Church
- ☐ Pastoral
- ☐ Prayer & Spirituality
- ☐ Resources for Children's Church
- ☐ Resources for Schools

Support your local bookshop
Ask about their new title information schemes.